I0157306

PRELIMINARY INVENTORY OF THE RECORDS OF THE POST OFFICE DEPARTMENT

Record Group 28

Compiled by
Arthur Hecht, Frank J. Nivert,
Fred W. Warriner, Jr., and Charlotte M. Ashby

Revised by
Forrest R. Holdcamper

HERITAGE BOOKS
2011

HERITAGE BOOKS

AN IMPRINT OF HERITAGE BOOKS, INC.

Books, CDs, and more—Worldwide

For our listing of thousands of titles see our website
at
www.HeritageBooks.com

A Facsimile Reprint
Published 2011 by
HERITAGE BOOKS, INC.
Publishing Division
100 Railroad Ave. #104
Westminster, Maryland 21157

Originally published

The National Archives
National Archives and Records Service
General Services Administration
Washington: 1967

National Archives Publication No. 68-1
Reprinted 1984

Library of Congress Catalog Card No. A67-7559

— Publisher's Notice —
In reprints such as this, it is often not possible to remove blemishes from the
original. We feel the contents of this book warrant its reissue despite these blemishes
and hope you will agree and read it with pleasure.

International Standard Book Numbers
Paperbound: 978-0-7884-3500-3
Clothbound: 978-0-7884-8668-5

CONTENTS

INTRODUCTION

The Office of the Postmaster General was established on July 26, 1775, with the appointment by the Continental Congress of Benjamin Franklin as Postmaster General for a term of 1 year. The position was continued by the Congress of the Confederation. Under the Federal Constitution, an act of September 22, 1789 (1 Stat. 70), provided for the temporary establishment of a General Post Office and authorized the appointment of a Postmaster General, who was subject to the direction of the President. The Postmaster General's duties, his salary, and the compensation paid to the assistant or clerk and to the deputy postmasters whom he appointed, as well as the regulations governing the Post Office Establishment, were to be the same as under the Congress of the Confederation. An act of February 20, 1792 (1 Stat. 232), provided in detail for the Post Office Department and the Postal Service. It gave the Postmaster General authority to appoint "an assistant, and deputy postmasters, at all places where such shall be found necessary." Subsequent acts made the Post Office Department a permanent agency and enlarged its duties.

The Post Office Department operated as a single, undifferentiated unit until the appointment of a Chief Clerk on April 1, 1818. The Chief Clerk was assigned supervision of field operations, including mail contracts, inspections, activities of the special agents and of the topographer, disbursements, and measures to deal with mail depredations. As the Post Office Department began to perform more services, other functions of the Postmaster General were delegated to the Chief Clerk and to an Assistant Postmaster General. In 1830 the Postmaster General became a regular member of the Cabinet.

Since 1946 the functions of the Office of the Postmaster General have been (1) supervising the Post Office Department; (2) appointing Post Office Department officers and employees (excluding the four Assistant Postmasters General and the Purchasing Agent, who, by acts of March 3, 1853, and April 28, 1904, respectively, are to be appointed by the President); (3) determining appeals from the decisions of the four Assistant Postmasters General; (4) issuing orders and promulgating rules and regulations concerning the organization and operation of the

Postal Service; and (5) considering claims for damage done through the operations of the Post Office Department and claims of postmasters for credit or reimbursement for losses from unavoidable mishaps, such as fire or burglary.

The Office of the Assistant Postmaster General was provided for under the Continental Congress and was continued under the Constitution. For many years the office was known as the Bureau of the First Assistant Postmaster General, but in 1950 its name was changed to the Bureau of Post Office Operations. The functions of the First Assistant Postmaster General were (1) the general management of post offices, including the rural delivery and special delivery services and the authorization of allowances for hiring clerks and city and village carriers; (2) establishing and discontinuing post offices, changing the names of post offices, and changing the sites of post offices of the fourth class; (3) bonding and commissioning postmasters, appointing postmasters at post offices of the fourth class, and selecting and nominating postmasters at post offices of the first, second, and third classes; and (4) handling matters concerning unmailable and undeliverable mail. The functions of the Bureau varied from time to time, however, and some functions were even interchanged among the other Assistant Postmasters General. Appendix I gives a detailed list of the First Assistant Postmaster General's functions, together with corresponding dates for each function. The records of the First Assistant Postmaster General described in this inventory are arranged according to the organization of the Bureau in 1946.

The position of Second Assistant Postmaster General was created by an act of April 30, 1810 (2 Stat. 593). Until November 15, 1851, the work of the Assistant Postmasters General was assigned on a geographical basis. On that date the Postmaster General assigned the work of his assistants on the basis of function, and the Second Assistant Postmaster General was made responsible for the transportation of mail. He supervised the letting of contracts for the transportation of mail and the mail messenger service. Reorganizations on August 1, 1891, and on December 1, 1905, broadened and strengthened his control over all phases of mail transportation.

As new means of transportation were developed, additional divisions and services were established in his office; in time the Office of the Second Assistant Postmaster General became known as a Bureau. In 1946 the Bureau was reorganized and on August 20, 1949, it was abolished. Its functions were continued by a Bureau of Transportation, headed by an Assistant Postmaster General.

Most of the records of the Bureau of the Second Assistant Postmaster General described in this inventory were created before the 1946 reorganization, and they are described within the organizational framework existing in the early part of 1946. At that time the Bureau's functions were (1) supervising the transportation of domestic and international mails by means of railroads, electric and cable cars, steam vessels, buses, trucks, or airplanes; (2) supervising the routing and distribution of the mail; (3) managing the international postal service; and (4) supervising the Bureau's administrative and budgetary services. For the development of the Bureau's organization from 1841 to 1950, see appendix II.

The position of the Third Assistant Postmaster General was established on July 2, 1836, and that of the Fourth Assistant Postmaster General on March 3, 1891. Although they had existed long before, the Bureau of Accounts was formally established in 1921 and the Bureau of the Chief Inspector in 1939, completing the pattern of bureau organization that survived until the Department was reorganized on August 30, 1949.

The records of the Post Office Department in the National Archives on July 1, 1967, amounted to 2,756 cubic feet and comprise Record Group 28, Records of the Post Office Department. They are described in this preliminary inventory, in which Forrest Holdcamper has revised and consolidated four earlier inventories: (1) Preliminary Inventory No. 36, Records of the Bureau of the First Assistant Postmaster General, 1789-1942, by Frank J. Nivert and Arthur Hecht; (2) Preliminary Inventory No. 82, Records of the Bureau of the Second Assistant Postmaster General, 1814-1946, by Arthur Hecht; (3) Preliminary Inventory No. 99, Records of the Office of the Postmaster General, by Arthur Hecht; and (4) Preliminary Inventory No. 114, Records of the Bureaus of the Third and Fourth Assistant Postmasters General, the Bureau of Accounts, and the Bureau of the Chief Inspector of the Post Office Department, by Arthur Hecht, Fred W. Warriner, Jr., and Charlotte M. Ashby.

The records of several original postal conventions are in Record Group 11, United States Government Documents Having General Legal Effect. Records relating to the postal service in Cuba, Puerto Rico, and the Philippines are in Record Group 140, Records of the Military Government of Cuba, and in Record Group 126, Records of the Office of Territories. Photographs illustrating the transportation of mail are in Record Group 111, Records of the Office of the Chief Signal Officer.

RECORDS OF THE IMMEDIATE OFFICE OF THE POSTMASTER GENERAL

1. ORDERS ("JOURNALS"). July 7, 1835-Mar. 5, 1953. 1,146 vols. 325 ft.

Copies of orders of the Postmaster General relating to the establishment, discontinuance, and reestablishment of post offices; changes in names and sites of post offices; appointments of postmasters; establishment and discontinuance of free delivery service, post office substations, distributing post offices, rural delivery offices, and money order stations; mail transportation; appointment, promotion, transfer, or resignation of employees; and violations of postal laws and regulations.

Also included among the orders are references to allowances for special services, compensation to postmasters and employees, departmental reorganizations, false returns by postmasters, invitations for bids for operating mail routes and furnishing equipment and supplies, international postal conventions, military postal services (in Cuba, the Philippine Islands, Puerto Rico, and France), telegraph and cable rates, changes in mail contracts, purchase of equipment and supplies, maintenance of post offices, and appointment of departmental committees to investigate the operations and administration of the Post Office Department.

Orders for the periods July 7, 1835, to July 1, 1867, and February 17, 1920, to March 5, 1953, are arranged chronologically. Orders for the period July 1, 1867, to February 18, 1920, are arranged by subject and thereunder chronologically. Described in entry 64 are other orders for the period July 1, 1867, to February 18, 1905, drafted by the First Assistant Postmaster General for the Postmaster General's signature and relating mainly to post offices and postmasters. Described in entry 51 is a register of "fraud orders" for the period November 1879 to June 30, 1951.

2. LETTERS SENT. Oct. 3, 1789-Dec. 31, 1910; May 22, 1912-Aug. 30, 1913; Jan. 1, 1915-Dec. 31, 1952. 502 vols. 90 ft.

Fair, press, and carbon copies of letters relating mainly to post offices, postmasters, mail transportation, mail contracts, departmental organizations, appropriations, budgetary matters, legislation, postal laws and regulations, international mail service, international postal conventions, postage stamps, personnel, mail frauds, lottery cases, and claims against the Post Office Department and postmasters. Each volume of the fair and press copies of letters up to May 28, 1908, contains an alphabetical index by name of correspondent or by subject. The letters are arranged chronologically.

3. DRAFTS OF LETTERS SENT. 1836-45. 1 ft.

Relate to the burning of the Post Office Department building, express mail, railroad mail service, mail contracts, postal deposits, Department expenditures, mail transportation to North Cumberland, post office clerks in Albany, the New Orleans post office, post offices in Indian territories, the appointment of Department employees, furniture and fixtures of the new Post Office Department building, postage costs, mail depredations, private mails, publication of foreign letters, newspaper controversies, mail robberies, dead letters, and to postmasters' accounts and the nomination, appointment, bonding, and compensation of postmasters. The drafts are arranged chronologically. Final copies of a few of the letters are among the records described in entry 2.

4. LETTERS RECEIVED. 1837-43. 1 ft.

Relate to quarterly accounts of postmasters; appointments of postmasters; postmasters' salaries; commissions, investigations, indictments, and dismissals of postmasters; sureties; mail service; claims against the Post Office Department; postal deposits; collection of claims; appointments and resignations of special agents; the franking privilege; recoveries of stolen postal funds; lost letters; postal advertisements; and drafts of payments to and from postmasters. Arranged by subject in the order listed and thereunder chronologically.

5. A FILM ENTITLED "THE STORY OF THE U.S. MAIL." n.d. 1 reel.

RECORDS OF THE OFFICE OF THE EXECUTIVE ASSISTANT TO THE POSTMASTER GENERAL

The position of Executive Assistant to the Postmaster General was established on January 29, 1930. The Executive Assistant performed such administrative duties as were assigned to him by the Postmaster General.

6. LETTERS SENT. Mar. 1, 1930-Nov. 5, 1935. 23 vols. 4 ft.

Carbon copies of letters sent mainly to Members of Congress. The letters relate to claims and complaints against the Post Office Department, rural and star mail routes, mail service, construction of Federal buildings, and appointment, transfer, and suspension of employees. Arranged chronologically.

RECORDS OF THE OFFICE OF THE ADMINISTRATIVE ASSISTANT TO THE POSTMASTER GENERAL

The position of Administrative Assistant to the Postmaster General was established about March 1, 1929. The duties of the Administrative Assistant were not specifically described but were assigned to him by the Postmaster General.

7. LETTERS SENT. July 11-Dec. 14, 1929. 1 vol. 2 in.

Carbon copies of replies of letters recommending individuals for the position of postmaster, complaints against postmasters, applications for the position of postmaster, and requests for the reinstatement of employees in the Post Office Department. Included are occasional references to mail transportation and commendations of postal employees retiring. Arranged chronologically.

RECORDS OF THE OFFICE OF THE CHIEF CLERK

The appointment of a Chief Clerk was authorized in April 1818. His duties were originally concerned with field and investigative activities of the Post Office Department. When the Department was organized in 1825 into three divisions, the Chief Clerk was placed in charge of the third division; and he supervised the Office of Mail Contracts (later the Inspection Office). From 1836 to 1872 he supervised the operations of the Division of Special Agents and Mail Depredations, the Office of the Topographer, the Office of the Superintendent of Buildings,

and the Disbursing Clerk. After the passage of the act of June 8, 1872 (17 Stat. 283), under which the Post Office Department operated for about 20 years, his functions gradually came to relate more and more to the administrative and operating activities of the Office of the Postmaster General.

The Chief Clerk became known as the Chief Clerk and Superintendent of Buildings on July 1, 1905, and as the Chief Clerk and Director of Personnel on July 1, 1934. He reviewed and prepared correspondence for the Postmaster General; promulgated and coordinated orders, circulars, and other matters between the bureaus and offices of the Post Office Department; and managed administrative activities such as personnel, payroll certificates, budgetary matters, printing, and the procurement of office equipment. The Chief Clerk also served as a member of the staff of the Postmaster General, was a member of the Council of Personnel Administration, represented the Department as a member of the Welfare and Recreational Association of Public Buildings and Grounds, Inc., and was a liaison officer between the Post Office Department and the Public Buildings Administration in matters relating to Department buildings and equipment.

8. ANNUAL REPORTS. 1836, 1840, 1846. 1 in.

Manuscript copies of annual reports of the Department, prepared by the Chief Clerk for the Postmaster General. Arranged chronologically.

9. CONGRESSIONAL CORRESPONDENCE AND RESOLUTIONS. 1839-41, 1854-58. 1 ft.

Letters and resolutions requesting data on the administration and operation of the Department (postal laws, postal routes, the franking privilege, names of employees, and fiscal matters) and copies of replies thereto. Several documents relating to the fortification of the Maine boundary are also included. Arranged by type of material as listed and thereunder chronologically.

10. LETTERS SENT. Jan. 18, 1873-Mar. 14, 1910. 117 vols. 11 ft.

Press copies of letters concerning employees, postmasters, telegraph rates for Government messages, appropriations, advertisements for services or supplies, second-class mail, repair and maintenance of post office buildings, and postal publications (postal guides, laws and regulations, annual reports, and post-route maps). Arranged chronologically. Each volume dated before July 11, 1905, includes an alphabetical index by name of correspondent.

11. RECORDS RELATING TO THE POST OFFICE DEPARTMENT BUILDING. 1827-55. 5 in.

Copies of deeds, leases, and memoranda, 1827, relating to buildings occupied by the Federal Government; correspondence concerning the burning of the Post Office Department building, 1836; correspondence, reports, lists, bids, contracts, and petitions relating to the construction of a new Post Office Department building, 1840-42; correspondence concerning the rental of temporary quarters at the Mansion House on 14th Street from Benjamin O. Tayloe, 1836-42, and his claims against the Government, 1842-50, for alleged lack of repairs to the building; and correspondence about the extension of the Post Office Department building, 1855. Arranged chronologically.

12. RECORDS OF THE OFFICE OF ELECTRO-MAGNETIC TELEGRAPH. 1837-46. 2 in.

Under an act of March 3, 1843, an experimental telegraph line from Washington to Baltimore was built and operated under the general direction of the Postmaster General, with Samuel F. B. Morse as superintendent. The line was constructed during 1843; was officially opened on May 24, 1844; and was turned over to private operation in December 1846. The records include correspondence of Samuel F. B. Morse and his assistants relating to the telegraphic system and the operation of the experimental line; drafts for money received; and copies of orders of the Postmaster General relating to the money allotted for the telegraph and to the setting of rates for it. Arranged chronologically.

13. AGREEMENTS ON TELEGRAPH RATES. 1866-1913. 1 ft.

Mainly rate agreements entered into with telegraph companies under an act of July 24, 1866, authorizing the Postmaster General to set rates for telegrams sent by the Government. Included is some related correspondence. Arranged alphabetically by company.

14. RECORDS RELATING TO TELEPHONIC AND TELEGRAPHIC SERVICES. July 6, 1906-Nov. 15, 1910; Jan. 1, 1911-Mar. 3, 1922. 3 vols. 3 in.

Orders, reports, and correspondence relating to the use of these services within the Post Office Department. Arranged chronologically.

For records relating to the use of the services for the period 1884-99, see entry 30.

15. NOTICES AND PROTESTED WARRANTS OF DRAFTS. 1837. 1 in.

These notices and protested warrants against payment of drafts on demand were received from postmasters at Albany, Baltimore, Boston, Clinton, Columbus, Hartford, Milledgeville, Mobile, Natchez, New Orleans, Newport, New York, Philadelphia, and Richmond. Arranged by name of post office and thereunder chronologically.

16. RECORDS RELATING TO THE CLAIM OF JOHN T. SULLIVAN FOR BINDING COPIES OF LAWS AND INSTRUCTIONS TO POSTMASTERS. 1939-48. 1 in.

Instructions, petitions, statements, and correspondence relating to the binding of 17,500 copies of postal laws and instructions to postmasters and to Mr. Sullivan's claim for reimbursement for the project. Arranged chronologically.

17. RECORDS OF THE CENSORSHIP BOARD. 1917-18. 40 ft.

The Censorship Board was established in 1917 under the direction of the Postmaster General and functioned until the end of the war. The records include correspondence relating to the personnel and operations of the Board. Arranged chronologically.

18. LETTERS RECOMMENDING JOHN ZUMSTEIN AS POSTMASTER FOR THE CINCINNATI, OHIO, POST OFFICE. Mar.-Aug. 1890. 3 vols. 3 in.

These letters, addressed to President Benjamin Harrison, were received from citizens of Cincinnati and from business firms and other organizations in the city. Arranged chronologically.

19. RECORDS RELATING TO THE KEEP COMMISSION. 1906-7. 1 vol. 3 in.

A commission headed by Charles H. Keep (Assistant Secretary of the Treasury) was appointed to investigate the business methods of executive agencies and to find ways to improve their administrative procedures. The commission was in operation from August 1905 to the end of December 1907. The records consist of carbon copies of 107 questions and answers concerning lines and divisions of responsibility in departmental organization or operation; duplication of work; use of committees; preparation of decisions for executive approval; appointments, salaries, and leave privileges of personnel; handling of correspondence; preservation of records; purchase, standardization, and testing of supplies; and methods of keeping and examining accounts. Arranged by office of the Post Office Department to which the records pertain.

20. FILMS SHOWING THE CONSTRUCTION OF THE POST OFFICE DEPARTMENT BUILD- ING IN WASHINGTON, D.C. 1931-34. 14 reels.

21. FILMS SHOWING SERVICES FURNISHED BY THE POST OFFICE DEPARTMENT AND METHODS USED IN SUPPLYING THEM. 1915-38. 51 reels.

22. FILMS SHOWING GERMAN AND ITALIAN VICTORIES IN FRANCE, POLAND, AND AT SEA. 1940-41. 32 reels.

The films were produced in Germany and circulated in other European countries for propaganda purposes.

RECORDS MAINTAINED BY THE APPOINTMENT CLERK

The position of Appointment Clerk was established about July 1, 1878. Under the direction of the Chief Clerk, he kept the official roster of all officers, clerks, and employees of the Department, including those employed at the stamp and official envelope agencies, post office inspectors, and superintendents and assistant superintendents of the Railway Mail Service; and he had charge of all papers, applications, recommendations, and files relating thereto. He certified the payrolls and prepared all the orders and correspondence relating to appointments, promotions, removals, and resignations.

23. REPORTS AND CORRESPONDENCE RE- LATING TO PERSONNEL. Jan. 9, 1904- May 26, 1913. 19 vols. and unbound papers. 3 ft.

Press copies of reports and correspondence relating to the appointment, transfer, promotion, absence, and separation of employees and to reductions in force. Included are personnel files for R. I. Hurd, composer of "Sweet Adeline," and for William S. Hart. The records are arranged chronologically.

RECORDS MAINTAINED BY THE MUSEUM

In the Museum of the Post Office Department, supervised by the Chief Clerk, were stored miscellaneous correspondence, early accounting

books, samples of forms, and equipment and other material used for exhibition purposes. Most of these records were transferred to the Library of Congress in 1905 and 1909 and from there to the National Archives in 1946. Some of the correspondence is described in entries 3 and 4 and 8-12. Other records held by the Museum are described below.

24. JOURNAL OF HUGH FINLAY, SURVEYOR OF POST ROADS AND POST OFFICES. Sept. 13, 1773-May 24, 1774. 1 vol. 1 in.

Mr. Finlay was appointed Surveyor of the Post Roads on the Continent of North America by the British Postmaster General on December 9, 1772. His proposals for improving postal service were approved and preparations were made to carry them out, but the Revolution intervened. Mr. Finlay's recommendations appear to have been known to Benjamin Franklin and were used by him when he established the General Post Office under the Continental Congress during the latter half of 1775.

This journal is a fair copy of Hugh Finlay's notes, containing information about the exploration of land from the Chaudière River in Canada to the first settlements on the Kennebec River; reports and comments about the post offices in the northern and southern districts of the North American Colonies; information about postmasters, post riders, and departure and arrival of mails at each post office; post office accounts; and surveys and sketches of possible mail routes.

25. MISCELLANEOUS RECORDS. 1794-1894. 1 ft.

A bond for Thomas Alexander, postmaster at Carlisle, Pa., dated April 15, 1794; Newbury, Vt., postage book, 1799-1801; schedules for mail routes Nos. 1204 and 1205, issued by the Contract Office on August 28, 1841; a report of a survey made in 1879 across Georgia and Florida by the U.S. Engineers, issued in 1881; postal accounting forms, 1855; forms used to keep statistics concerning mail between the United States and Bremen, undated; receipts used by the French post office department, undated; rates of postage in the countries forming the German Postal Union, undated; Chinese or Japanese postal pamphlets, undated; postal forms used by the British Empire, 1850-60; statements of railway mail service in Great Britain and Ireland in 1854; a pamphlet entitled Stage Coaches and Railroads or the Past and the Present of Transportation Facilities, from Nashville, Through Tennessee, Kentucky and Surrounding Territory, Showing the Difference Between Then and Now, and the Advantages of Railroads to All

Classes; and postmasters' account and record books from Emahaka, Ind., 1898-1903, Peru, Ind., 1905-6, and Holdenville (Indian Territory), 1898-1908; money order records of Mobile, Ala., 1864-67; and commissions of the postmaster in Berlin, Ky., 1868. Arranged by type of record as listed.

26. RECORD OF LETTERS SENT FROM THE WILMINGTON, DEL., POST OFFICE TO OTHER POST OFFICES. Mar. 10, 1786-June 11, 1792. 1 vol. 2 in.

Shows date each letter was sent and its destination; the number of unpaid, paid, and free letters; and sums paid and unpaid. The entries are arranged chronologically.

27. SCRAPBOOK OF CIRCULARS, NOTICES, INSTRUCTIONS, REGULATIONS, AND NEWSPAPER CLIPPINGS. 1823-71. 1 vol. 2 in.

The circulars and notices relate to the franking privilege, type of mail handled, postage stamps, postage rates, express mail, establishment of post offices, political activities of personnel, private mail service, transportation of mail by way of the Isthmus of Panama, safety of mail service on railroads, railway mail cars, changes in mail routes and schedules, mail-route contracts, mail locks and keys, military mail service, mutilated U.S. currency, and the method of handling inquiries. The instructions and regulations relate to the reorganization of the Post Office Department, private mail service, railway mail-route contracts, dead letters, registration of postage stamps and stamped envelopes, abolishment of payment of commissions to postmasters, mail-route carriers, conveyance of mailbags to Members of Congress, activities of route agents, and the franking privilege. The clippings are chiefly editorials and letters to the editor concerning the postal system but also include news items containing information of research value about the growth of the system, such as information on the distribution of anti-slavery publications, the operations of Pomeroy & Co. (private mail carriers), and irregularities allegedly committed by postal officials. Also included in the scrapbook are the petition of citizens of the County of Herkimer, N.Y., for a reduction in postage rates; orders of the Postmaster General concerning office hours, uniform postage rates between the United States and Canada, and suspension of mail service in the Southern States; forms used by the Contract Office, the Appointment Office, and the Office of the Auditor of the Treasury for the Post Office Department; memorials for the transportation of foreign mail by steamship; and advertisements for contracts for steam mail service between New York and New Orleans.

28. RECORD OF MAILS SENT AND RECEIVED AT THE COLLINS, ERIE COUNTY, N.Y., POST OFFICE. 1827-29. 1 vol. 1 in.

This volume is primarily a register and account book. The entries are arranged alphabetically by name of post office to which each letter was sent.

RECORDS OF THE DISBURSING OFFICER

An act of March 3, 1853 (10 Stat. 211), authorized the appointment of a Disbursing Clerk for the Post Office Department. His title was later changed to Superintendent of the Post Office Building and Disbursing Officer (or Clerk) by an act of June 8, 1872 (17 Stat. 283). The position was transferred to the Office of the Third Assistant Postmaster General in accordance with an appropriation act of June 19, 1878 (20 Stat. 178). By an order of the Postmaster General dated August 1, 1891, the Office of the Superintendent of the Post Office Building and Disbursing Clerk was established as a separate unit. On November 1, 1905, the Postmaster General changed the title of the official in charge to the Disbursing Officer. On November 15, 1943, he was redesignated the Director of Postal Finance, Bureau of the Third Assistant Postmaster General. His functions are now performed within the Bureau of Finance.

These functions in 1946 included the maintenance of buildings and equipment, the purchase of supplies, the disbursement of salaries and of money for other expenditures, the publication of the Official Guide, the sale of wastepaper and unserviceable property, and the maintenance of accounts relating to these activities.

29. LETTERS SENT. 1862-87. 5 vols. 5 in.

Press copies of outgoing letters relating to contingent expenses, issuance of warrants, payment of vouchers, salary payments, sale of wastepaper, purchase of equipment and supplies for the Post Office Department Building, price-lists, and orders for post-route maps. Arranged chronologically.

30. GENERAL RECORDS. 1884-99, 1911-13. 2 ft.

A representative sample of the records that were destroyed. Arranged in three chronological groups as follows: (1) receipts for sales of wastepaper and unserviceable property (jute, scrap leather, burlap, canvas, cord, drums, shears, wire, catchers, iron and steel scrap, and carboys), 1911-13; (2) correspondence, statements, vouchers, contracts, and lists relating to the use of telephone and telegraph service by the Post Office Department, 1884-99; and (3) press copies of requisitions, 1885-86. For additional records concerning the telephonic and telegraphic services, see entry 14.

31. RECORDS RELATING TO THE POST OF-
FICE DEPARTMENT BUILDING. 1871-75, 1893. 2 vols. 2 in.

One volume consists of an 1871-75 property inventory of equipment and furniture in each room of the Post Office Department Building located at 8th and E Streets, NW., Washington, D.C. The other volume contains an 1893 report by S. T. G. Morsell, a measurer appointed by the Interior Department in connection with the painting of walls, ceilings, and cases. This report shows the measurements of each room, corridor, and stairway in the Post Office Department Building. The entries in the first volume are arranged chronologically.

RECORDS OF THE PRIVATE SECRETARY TO THE POSTMASTER GENERAL

Postmaster General A. W. Randall was the first to appoint a third-class clerk to act as his secretary. Officially referred to as "stenographer" from July 1, 1873, to August 1, 1899, and after that as "private secretary," the position was equivalent to that of an administrative assistant. The Postmaster General assigned him tasks at his discretion.

32. LETTERS SENT. Dec. 18, 1867-June 26, 1874; May 29, 1893-Dec. 31, 1895; May 1, 1897-Dec. 27, 1901. 13 vols. 2 ft.

Press copies of letters relating to the employment of clerks and postmasters; military postal service; postal service inventions; the establishment of post offices and rural free delivery service; the establishment of a postal savings system; and postal service in Cuba, the Philippine Islands, and Puerto Rico. Arranged chronologically.

RECORDS OF THE DIVISION OF SERVICE RELATIONS

The Postal Employees' Cooperative Store Association, located in the Post Office Department Building, Washington, D.C., was organized during the fall of 1917 to operate a store to sell groceries and other items at wholesale prices. Its board of 16 directors represented every office and bureau of the Post Office Department.

The cooperative was dissolved on January 14, 1921; its funds were distributed to the members; and its records were turned over to the Chief Clerk of the Department.

On April 21, 1921, the Post Office Department established a Welfare Division, later known as the Division of Service Relations. Through national, county, local, and departmental councils, it developed programs for health improvement, hospitalization, education, improved sanitary and working conditions, economic self-help, and cooperation between officials and their subordinates.

33. GENERAL RECORDS OF THE POSTAL
EMPLOYEES' COOPERATIVE STORE AS-
SOCIATION. 1917-21. 3 in.

Mainly minutes of the board of directors. Included are the constitution of the association, statements of receipts and expenditures, and pricelists. Arranged by type of record and thereunder chronologically.

34. GENERAL RECORDS OF THE DIVISION
OF SERVICE RELATIONS. 1921-30. 3 in.

Minutes of meetings of the National Service Relations Council; correspondence of the Post Office Department Service Council concerning the welfare of employees; biographical sketches of members of the Welfare Council; petitions of Philadelphia postal employees for a cafeteria in the post office building; notices and announcements of activities of the Welfare Board; news items for the publication Postal Spirit, and copies of the Postal Spirit. Arranged by type of record and thereunder chronologically.

RECORDS OF THE OFFICE OF THE SOLICITOR

On May 8, 1794, a solicitor was appointed by the Postmaster General to take charge of contracts and other legal matters. When the Post Office Establishment was organized into three divisions in 1825, the solicitor was included in the first division. An act of June 1, 1872, authorized the Postmaster General to appoint as his chief law officer an Assistant Attorney General for the Post Office Department, and the first incumbent of the office was appointed on March 20, 1873. All evidence obtained from investigations of alleged operation through the mails of lotteries and fraudulent enterprises was reviewed by the Assistant Attorney General before being acted upon by the Postmaster General. The Assistant Attorney General was paid from the appropriations of the Department of Justice; but, beginning in 1878, he was provided with a staff from the appropriations for the Post Office Department. His title was changed to Solicitor for the Post Office Department by an act of June 16, 1914 (38 Stat. 454).

An act of July 28, 1916 (39 Stat. 412), authorized the appointment by the Postmaster General of a Special Assistant to the Attorney General, and the position was provided for by postal appropriations from 1917 to 1934. This official assisted "in the defense of cases against the United States arising out of the transportation of the mails, and in other cases and matters affecting the postal revenues." In 1934 the Office of the Special Assistant to the Attorney General and the Office of the Solicitor for the Post Office Department were merged to form the Office of the Solicitor of the Post Office Department. Thereafter the appropriations for this Office were disbursed by the Post Office Department.

The functions delegated to the Office by the Postmaster General included drafting bills for Congress, amendments to postal laws and regulations, and legal opinions; preparing reports on legislation pertaining to the Department; representing the Postmaster General before regulatory commissions; settling claims against the Department; passing upon the legality of contracts involving the Department; trying cases resulting from alleged use of the mails to defraud; assisting in the defense of cases against the Federal Government arising from postal activities; and considering applications for executive clemency for persons violating postal laws.

CENTRAL NUMERIC FILE

In 1905 the Office of the Assistant Attorney General for the Post Office Department established a numeric file in which most records were to be maintained. Records relating to a single activity were put in a case file, which was assigned a serial number. At the time the individual case files were organized, a register of transactions and subject cards were prepared to serve as an index to the series. This system was continued by the successors to the Assistant Attorney General until 1951, when a new filing system was adopted.

In 1934 most records relating to Federal operation of telephone, telegraph, and cable companies for the period 1918-21 were withdrawn from the series and transferred to the newly created Federal Communications Commission (see entry 38). In 1944 another segment relating to the enforcement of the Espionage Act during World War I was transferred to the National Archives (see entry 40). The segments described in entries 36 and 41-46 were also transferred to the National Archives. In 1953 the Post Office Department and the National Archives reappraised these records for the purpose of eliminating those of negligible research value. Acting under congressional authorization, they disposed of most of the files. (For a sampling, see entry 36.)

35. CARD INDEX TO GENERAL RECORDS. 1905-21. 3 ft.
These 5" x 8" cards show the name of the violator of a postal law or regulation, type of violation, law or regulation violated, and case number. Arranged alphabetically by name of violator.

36. GENERAL RECORDS. 1905-21. 10 ft.
Selected case files consisting chiefly of correspondence, memoranda, postal inspectors' reports, and exhibits (mainly copies of publications) relating to cases involving the use of the mails for fraud, sedition, lotteries, false advertising, and obscene matter, and other violations of postal laws and regulations. Also included are some records relating to the organization and administration of the Office. Arranged by case number.

37. CARD INDEX TO RECORDS RELATING TO FEDERAL OPERATION OF TELEPHONE, TELEGRAPH, AND CABLE COMPANIES. 1919-21. 12 ft.
These 4" x 6" cards show the original registry numbers of the records described in entry 38. Arranged alphabetically by subject.

38. RECORDS RELATING TO FEDERAL OPERATION OF TELEPHONE, TELEGRAPH, AND CABLE COMPANIES. 1918-21. 12 ft.
These records document Federal control of communication systems under a joint congressional resolution of July 16, 1918, and a Presidential proclamation of July 22, 1918, authorizing the Postmaster General to supervise the operation of all telephone, telegraph, and cable companies. The companies continued to operate the facilities as agents of the Government until January 1, 1919, when the Postmaster General established a Board of Operations within the United States Telegraph and Telephone Administration to manage the facilities. The facilities were returned to their owners on July 31, 1919, and the Postmaster General determined the rate of compensation due each company. The Solicitor handled the resulting litigation, and he inherited and organized all the records of Federal operation. In 1934 the records were transferred

to the Federal Communications Commission and, later, to the National Archives. Included in the records are studies and reports on private operation of various communication systems; orders, correspondence, memoranda, reports, circulars, bulletins, and publicity materials relating to Federal operation; and dockets relating to the settlement of the compensatory claims. Arranged by type of record.

39. CARD RECORDS RELATING TO FEDERAL OPERATION OF TELEPHONE, TELE-GRAPH, AND CABLE COMPANIES. 1919-21. 13 ft.

On 3" x 5" and 5" x 8" cards. The cards are arranged alphabetically in seven groups as follows: (1) names and addresses of telephone, telegraph, and cable companies; (2) names and addresses of holding and subsidiary companies; (3) data on income and depreciation for individual firms; (4) names of companies submitting reports and completed questionnaires; (5) data on rate changes for individual firms; (6) names of cities in which companies were located; and (7) names of Members of Congress with whom the Post Office Department corresponded regarding the program.

40. RECORDS RELATING TO THE ESPIONAGE ACT, WORLD WAR I. 1917-21. 94 ft.

Case files relating to the denial of second-class mailing privileges to periodicals and other publications under section 12 of the Espionage Act of June 15, 1917 (40 Stat. 217). The act provided that any matter advocating treason, insurrection, or forcible resistance to any law of the United States was nonmailable. Included in the files are opinions interpreting the act. Part of the case files are arranged numerically.

41. RECORDS RELATING TO THE ESPIONAGE ACT, WORLD WAR II. 1942-45. 25 ft.

Case files similar to those described in entry 40, pertaining to the denial of mailing privileges to certain publications. Arranged by case number.

42. RECORDS RELATING TO AIRMAIL AND OCEAN-MAIL CONTRACTS. 1934-40. 32 ft.

Records relating to an investigation of airmail and ocean-mail contracts in 1933-35 by a special committee of the Senate, to hearings held by the Postmaster General and his subordinates on such contracts in accordance with an Executive order of July 11, 1934, and to the subsequent altering or canceling of the contracts. Included are interdepartmental and congressional correspondence relating to investigations; reports, studies, statistical tabulations, and accounting materials containing detailed data on the operation of numerous air- and ocean-transport companies; correspondence and publications criticizing contracts; postal inspectors' reports on contracts; applications, bids, authorizations, orders, decisions, and other materials relating to negotiations on contracts; dossiers relating to airmail rate proceedings before the Inter-state Commerce Commission; and reports on the classification of ocean-mail contract vessels. In two groups, each arranged by case number. For transcripts of the hearings, see entry 53.

43. CORRESPONDENCE AND MEMORANDA RELATING TO THE ADMISSIBILITY OF FOREIGN PUBLICATIONS. 1940-47. 1 ft.
Arranged chronologically.

44. BRIEFS OF CONTENTS OF NONMAILABLE PUBLICATIONS. 1940-47. 9 ft.
Arranged by number, 0001-07551.

45. LISTS OF MAILABLE AND NONMAILABLE PUBLICATIONS. 1940-47. 6 ft.
Arranged alphabetically by title of publication.

46. CASE FILE RELATING TO ESQUIRE MAGAZINE. 1943-46. 10 ft.

The official documentation relating to the attempt by the Postmaster General to revoke the second-class mailing privileges of Esquire on charges of obscenity, and the magazine's successful appeal to the courts to overrule him. The file includes complaints against the periodical, reports and findings of the Department, transcripts of the judicial proceedings, exhibits, and related correspondence. Arranged by type of record.

OTHER RECORDS

47. OFFICE FILES OF WILLIAM H. LAMAR. 1912-22. 8 in.

Mr. Lamar served as Special Assistant Attorney General and later as Solicitor for the Post Office Department. His files include papers relating to Federal operation of the telegraph and telephone systems; minutes of the Twenty-First Annual Convention of the National Association of Postmasters, 1921; applications and correspondence relating to the recruitment of translators; and miscellaneous materials concerning the use of the mails by certain publications. Arranged by type of record.

48. OPINIONS. 1868-74, 1895-97. 3 in.

Relate chiefly to the denial of mailing privileges of certain periodicals and pamphlets, and to lotteries, loss of mail, accounting for funds of the Department, disposal of stamps, issuance of postal cards, the franking privilege, investment schemes investigated by the Department, installation of pneumatic tubes, and liabilities of the Department in connection with delays in delivering mail. The opinions for the period 1895-97 are in the form of copies of outgoing letters, numbered 1482-1572. Arranged chronologically.

49. LETTERS SENT. Feb. 1877-Mar. 1879; July-Aug. 1906. 2 vols. 3 in.

Press copies of outgoing letters relating to changes in postal laws, mail contracts, the classification of second-class mailing matter, Southern ante bellum claims, franking-privilege fraud orders, applications for pardons, claims for rewards, and monthly work reports. Arranged chronologically.

50. "FRAUD ORDER CASE FILES." 1834-79, 1881-96, 1912-47. 79 ft.

Relate mainly to the use of the mails to send fraudulent advertisements, lotteries, and obscene matter. Each file includes a report on findings, a statement on the application of laws and regulations to the case, the recommendation and order of the Postmaster General, and the acknowledgment of receipt of the order by the local postmaster to whom the mail was delivered. Included in some case files are applications to restore mailing privileges or applications for executive clemency. Also included are case files relating to claims by private citizens for damages resulting from postal operations. Arranged by case number.

51. REGISTER OF "FRAUD ORDERS." Nov. 1879-June 30, 1951. 8 vols. 5 ft.

The orders forbade postmasters to pay any postal money orders to transmit mail for specific violators of postal laws and regulations. The orders are arranged numerically, 1-9199. Some similar service orders are described in entry 1.

52. TRANSCRIPTS OF HEARINGS ON FRAUD CASES. 1913-45. 63 ft.

Relate to some of the cases described in entry 50, chiefly those concerned with fraudulent stock, real estate ventures, and quackery. Arranged by serial number, 1-280. A transcript of the proceedings in United States v. George E. Lorenz, Martha J. Lorenz, August W. Machen, Diller B. Groff, and Samuel A. Groff (1904), relating to frauds perpetrated by Post Office employees, is at the beginning of the series.

53. TRANSCRIPTS OF HEARINGS ON AIRMAIL AND OCEAN-MAIL CONTRACTS. Oct.-Dec. 1934. 7 ft.

The hearings, called to consider the cancellation of certain contracts, relate to the 1933-35 investigation referred to in entry 42. The transcripts are arranged chronologically.

54. DOCKET OF CASES REFERRED TO THE ASSISTANT ATTORNEY GENERAL FOR THE POST OFFICE DEPARTMENT. 1886-90. 1 vol. 1 in.

Includes the name and date of each case, the name of the departmental unit from whom the case was received, and comments about its disposition. The entries are arranged chronologically.

55. FRAUD DOCKETS. 1900-July 1951. 22 vols. 3 ft.

Contain the names of the defendants involved in postal law violations, names of their attorneys, and digests of correspondence relating to the cases. Arranged chronologically.

56. DOCKETS OF STATE AND FEDERAL DISTRICT COURT CASES INVOLVING POSTAL LAWS. July 1917-July 1951. 4 vols. 8 in.

Relate mainly to lotteries and to matters of obscenity. Arranged by State or district court and thereunder chronologically.

57. REGISTERS OF POSTMASTERS' CLAIMS. 1882-1929. 19 vols. 3 ft.

Prepared in connection with the administration of the act of March 17, 1882 (22 Stat. 29), authorizing the Postmaster General to credit or reimburse postmasters for the loss of money order funds, postage stamps, and other stamped paper under circumstances such as fire, theft, or flood. Each register entry includes the name and address of the postmaster, cause of the loss, and a comment about the disposition of the claim. Arranged chronologically.

58. SURETY BONDS ("JUSTIFICATIONS"). 1901-2, 1908. 8 in.

Mainly justifications issued by the United States Fidelity & Guarantee Corporation for bonding mail-route carriers. Each justification includes the name of the bonded individual and, usually, a reference to his assigned route. Also included are samples of bonds used in other units of the Department, which were sent to the

Assistant Attorney General in accordance with Postmaster General's Order No. 1821 of October 20, 1908. Arranged chronologically.

RECORDS OF THE OFFICE OF THE PURCHASING AGENT

An act of April 28, 1904 (33 Stat. 429), authorized the President to appoint a Purchasing Agent to coordinate and supervise all procurement programs of the Department.

59. LETTERS SENT. May-Dec. 1904, Jan.-Mar. 1910, June-Dec. 1910. 9 vols. 1 ft.
   Press copies of outgoing letters relating to the purchase of supplies and equipment and their specifications, changes in contracts, and advertisements for bids. The letters are arranged chronologically. Each volume includes an index to the names of the correspondents. Records relating to the purchase of furniture for rural post offices from Waddel Wooden Ware Works are at the end of the series.

RECORDS OF THE BUREAU OF THE FIRST ASSISTANT POSTMASTER GENERAL

RECORDS OF THE IMMEDIATE OFFICE OF THE FIRST ASSISTANT POSTMASTER GENERAL

60. LETTERS SENT. Oct. 27, 1793-Mar. 26, 1800. 3 vols. 3 in.
   Handwritten copies of letters sent by the First Assistant Postmaster General relating to contracts for new mail routes and post roads, to mail contracts, and to payment of salaries to postmasters. The volumes were originally marked "A," "B," and "C." Volumes "A" and "B" are also marked "Assistant Postmaster General" and volume "C" is marked "First Assistant." The letters are arranged chronologically.

61. MISCELLANEOUS CORRESPONDENCE. 1911-28, 1929-32. 8 in.
   Correspondence of Arch Coleman, First Assistant Postmaster General, 1929-32, relating to semiofficial matters including political activities, speeches, trips, publicity, and relations with other Government officials; and correspondence regarding salaries, promotions, and an overall war plan. Arranged in three chronological groups.

62. STATEMENTS RELATING TO POST OFFICE DEPARTMENT APPROPRIATION BILLS AND OTHER LEGISLATION. 1912-31. 1 ft.
   Through the Division of Post Office Service, the First Assistant Postmaster General prepared advisory statements for the Postmaster General concerning proposed legislation affecting Department personnel. These statements relate to such subjects as salary increases, overtime pay, retirement, and leave. Included is some correspondence with Members of Congress regarding postal service appointments. Arranged by subject.

63. CORRESPONDENCE AND REPORTS RELATING TO CREDIT UNIONS FOR POSTAL EMPLOYEES. 1923-41. 6 ft.
   As part of its employee-relations program, the Department--under its Service Relations Office in the Office of the Postmaster General from 1923 to 1935 and thereafter under the First Assistant Postmaster General--sponsored and assisted the development of credit unions for postal employees. The records consist of correspondence and reports of postmasters, credit union officers, postal inspectors, and others regarding the development and control of credit unions. Arranged alphabetically by State and thereunder by city.

64. ORDERS ("JOURNALS"). July 1867-Feb. 1905. 71 vols. 21 ft.
   Handwritten copies of orders written by the First Assistant Postmaster General for the Postmaster General's signature. The orders show dates of appointment and salaries of letter carriers in the city delivery service; dates of establishment and discontinuance of post offices and changes in their names and sites; and names of postmasters appointed and the persons they replaced. Similar orders are found in the journals of the Postmaster General from July 1835 to June 1867 (see entry 1). After February 20, 1905, all orders of the Postmaster General, regardless of the Assistant's office where they were written, were bound together. The journal entries are arranged chronologically.

65. REPORTS AND CORRESPONDENCE RELATING TO CONVENTIONS OF POSTMASTERS. 1908-9, 1922-28. 7 in.
   Copies of reports and correspondence relating to the attendance of the Superintendent of the Division at regional and State conventions of postal officials (see also entry 66). Arranged in part alphabetically by State where convention was held.

66. REPORTS RELATING TO CONVENTIONS OF POSTMASTERS. 1922-27. 5 in.

Mainly reports, with related correspondence and exhibits, from postal inspectors who represented the Department at regional and State conventions of postal officials (see also entry 65). Arranged alphabetically by State where convention was held.

RECORDS OF THE DIVISION OF POSTMASTERS

67. RECORD OF FIRST RETURNS RECEIVED FROM POSTMASTERS. Oct. 1789-July 1818. 1 vol. 4 in.

Postmasters were required to submit quarterly statements of their accounts ("returns") to the Postmaster General. This volume, marked "All States and Territories 1790-1820," was apparently prepared from accounts of postmasters after the original record was burned in a fire in 1836. It contains names of post offices and States where located, names of postmasters, and dates when postmasters' first returns were received by the Postmaster General. The names of postmasters are frequently misspelled and there are other inaccuracies. By referring to the volumes described in entry 68 and to the letter books of the Postmaster General and accounts current, the actual dates of appointments of postmasters from 1789 to about 1800 can be found. The returns are arranged alphabetically by first letter of name of post office and thereunder by State.

68. RECORD OF APPOINTMENT OF POST-MASTERS. 1815-32. 6 vols. 2 ft.

The volumes are numbered 2-7. Volume 2 is divided into three parts: (1) the names of post offices in operation in 1814, arranged alphabetically, (2) the names of post offices inadvertently omitted from the first group, and (3) the names of post offices established from 1815 to 1818, arranged by date of establishment. For each post office are given the name and date of appointment of each postmaster, the number assigned to the post office by the Postmaster General, any changes in the name of the post office, the date of discontinuance, the amount of the surety bond, and the date of any changes in the bond.

Volume 3 is divided into two parts: (1) the names of post offices in operation in 1818, arranged alphabetically, and (2) the names of post offices established from 1818 to 1823, arranged by date of establishment or change in name. In addition to the types of information concerning each post office that are given in Volume 2, this volume gives the names of sureties. (The first part of this volume also gives, for each post office, the name of the last postmaster listed in Volume 2.)

Volume 4 is divided into two parts: (1) the names of post offices in operation in 1824, arranged alphabetically, and (2) the names of post offices established from 1825 to 1827, arranged by date of establishment. In addition to the types of information concerning each post office that are given in Volume 3, this volume gives the name of the county in which each post office is located.

Volume 5 is divided into two parts: (1) the names of all post offices in operation in 1827, arranged alphabetically, and (2) the names of post offices established from January 1827 to October 1828, arranged by date of establishment. This volume gives the same types of information concerning each post office as are given in volume 4.

Volumes 6 and 7 are arranged by the first letter of the name of the post office, A-L and M-Z, respectively. Under each letter, post offices in existence in 1828 are arranged alphabetically, followed by post offices established from 1828 to 1832, arranged by date of establishment. In addition to the same types of information concerning each post office as are given in volume 4, these two volumes give the dates of name changes for many post offices.

69. RECORD OF APPOINTMENT OF POST-MASTERS. 1832-1930. 98 vols. 33 ft.

The volumes, which are numbered 8 to 101, have been rebound so that there are now 98 volumes. Included in the information given are names of postmasters for each post office and dates of their appointments; dates of discontinuance, reestablishment, and name changes of post offices; dates of Presidential appointments of postmasters and dates of their confirmation by the Senate; usually, dates post offices were authorized to issue money orders; and, occasionally, dates of changes in location or site. Until 1844 the names of sureties for postmasters and the dates and amounts of their bonds are given. The records are arranged in the approximate periods 1832-42, 1843-57, 1858-73, 1874-89, and 1890-1930; thereunder by name of State or territory in rough alphabetical order; thereunder by name of county; and thereunder by name of post office. A penciled list shows the volume numbers for each State. An index by name of post office is described in entry 72. See also entries 70 and 71.

70. RECORD OF THE COMMISSIONING AND
APPOINTMENT OF POSTMASTERS.
1889-1908. 68 vols. 21 ft.

The record appears to have been compiled
under the Office of the Fourth Assistant Postmaster General from 1889 to 1906 in connection
with the bonding and commissioning of postmasters. In 1906 this function was transferred
to the First Assistant Postmaster General, and
after a short time the record was discontinued.
The record contains names, dates of appointment, commissions, and salaries of postmasters;
names of post offices; names of counties where
located; dates of establishment, discontinuance,
and reestablishment; name and site changes;
and dates of establishment of rural delivery
service where post offices were discontinued.
Arranged alphabetically by State and thereunder
by post office. The volumes include some information not contained in the series described
in entry 69 and should be used in conjunction
with that series.

71. DAILY RECORD OF THE APPOINTMENT
OF POSTMASTERS AND OF THE ESTAB-
LISHMENT, DISCONTINUANCE, AND
NAME AND SITE CHANGES OF POST OF-
FICES. Jan. 1899-Dec. 1914. 42 vols.
12 ft.

For each post office where a change occur-
red the following information is given: its name,
county and State where located, names of postmaster appointed and of postmaster retiring,
cause of change, and other remarks concerning
postmasters. From 1889 to 1905 these volumes
were prepared in the Office of the Fourth Assistant Postmaster General; in 1906 the function
was assumed by the First Assistant Postmaster
General. Arranged chronologically.

72. INDEX TO THE RECORD OF APPOINT-
MENT OF POSTMASTERS. 1840-1908.
27 vols. 9 ft.

The volume for 1840-54 includes names of
post offices in all States and territories with the
exception of Maryland, Ohio, Michigan, and the
New England and the Middle Atlantic States;
later volumes include names of post offices in
all States and territories in existence at the time
of compilation. The volumes through 1876 give
name changes and frequently dates of reestablishment and discontinuance; later volumes give
only names of post offices. This series can be
used as an index to part of the records described
in entry 69, if the name of the post office is
known. The records are arranged in the periods
1840-54, 1855-69, 1870-76, 1877-91, and
1892-1908; and thereunder alphabetically by
name of post office.

73. ALPHABETICAL RECORD OF APPOINT-
MENT OF POSTMASTERS IN IOWA,
LOUISIANA, ARKANSAS, AND MISSOURI.
("INDEX TO POST OFFICES"). 1866-74.
2 vols. 6 in.

An incomplete record that can be used in
conjunction with entries 69 and 72. Each entry
contains the names, changes in names, and dates
of discontinuance of post offices and the names,
dates of appointment, and salaries of postmasters.
Arranged alphabetically by name of post office.

74. MISCELLANEOUS RECORDS REGARDING
THE APPOINTMENT AND REAPPOINTMENT
OF POSTMASTERS. 1907-13. 1 ft.

Correspondence, reports, and memoranda
pertaining to the qualifications of applicants; and
petitions, applications, and other records relating to the service of incumbent postmasters.
Arranged alphabetically by State and thereunder
by city.

75. CORRESPONDENCE WITH MEMBERS OF
CONGRESS CONCERNING ACTING POST-
MASTERS. 1923-24. 1 in.

Relates to the appointment of acting postmasters as postmasters. Arranged in two
groups, for 1923 and 1924.

76. REPORTS OF CIVIL SERVICE COMMISSION
INVESTIGATIONS OF APPLICATIONS FOR
POSTMASTERSHIPS. 1918-21. 4 ft.

Summaries and verbatim reports of inter-
views conducted with legislators and prominent
citizens concerning the qualifications of candidates
for postmasterships. Arranged alphabetically by
State.

77. EXHIBITS RELATING TO THE CASE OF
POSTMASTER JOHN A. THORNTON OF
PHILADELPHIA. 1915-21. 2 ft.

Correspondence, reports, notes, and affidavits collected in the investigation of charges
of political activity and favoritism against Postmaster Thornton. Arranged in the order listed.

RECORDS OF THE DIVISION OF
POST OFFICE CLERICAL SERVICE

78. RECORD OF SALARIES OF REGULAR
CLERKS AND OTHER PERSONNEL IN
FIRST- AND SECOND-CLASS POST OFFICES.
July 1, 1889-June 30, 1907. 28 vols. 6 ft.

For each post office the record contains the
name of each clerk, his title, salary, date of
appointment, and date of separation or other
change in status. Each volume is indexed by
name of post office. The volumes for 1896-1907
are numbered from 1 to 24; the others are not

numbered. Arranged within the periods 1889-96, 1896-99, 1899-1904, and 1904-7; thereunder alphabetically by name of post office; and thereunder, for large offices, alphabetically by name of clerk, or, for small offices, chronologically by date of appointment.

79. RECORD OF APPOINTMENT OF SUBSTITUTE CLERKS IN THE FIRST- AND SECOND-CLASS POST OFFICES. July 1, 1899-June 30, 1905. 2 vols. 3 in.

For each post office the record contains the name of the substitute clerk, date of his appointment to that position, date of his appointment as a regular clerk, and notations concerning any other changes in his status. Arranged alphabetically by name of post office and thereunder by date of appointment.

80. RECORD CARDS OF SECOND-CLASS POST OFFICES. 1916-25. 3 in.

Each card gives date of establishment of post office. Some of the cards also give the date of establishment of city delivery service. Arranged alphabetically by city or town.

81. RECORDS RELATING TO CONTRACT STATIONS AND BRANCHES. 1916-35. 53 ft.

Included are bids for contract stations, recommendations of postmasters, reports of postal inspectors, copies of contracts (some signed), petitions, complaints, notices, correspondence, and other material relating to the establishment, operation, and discontinuance of contract post office stations. These stations were usually in large cities or their suburbs and were operated on a contract basis. Arranged alphabetically by State and thereunder by city.

82. REPORTS RELATING TO SUNDAY SERVICE AND THE NEED FOR ADDITIONAL PERSONNEL. 1911-12. 2 ft.

Reports received from the postmasters at certain large post offices regarding the operation of Sunday service and the number of additional personnel needed to make the 8-hour-day law operable. Some of the reports also give detailed statements concerning the operation of post offices. Arranged alphabetically by State and thereunder by city.

83. CORRESPONDENCE WITH THIRD-CLASS POST OFFICES. 1925-36. 3 in.

Relates to the operation of the post offices, with particular emphasis on the annual allowances for hiring clerks. Arranged in rough chronological order.

RECORDS OF THE DIVISION OF CITY DELIVERY SERVICE

84. RECORD CARDS OF CARRIERS SEPARATED FROM THE POSTAL SERVICE. 1863-99. 12 ft.

Each card, 3" x 5", contains name of post office, name of carrier, date of appointment, reason for separation, and, after 1873, date of separation. Arranged alphabetically by post office and thereunder by name of carrier.

85. REGISTER OF REGULAR CARRIERS IN FIRST- AND SECOND-CLASS POST OFFICES. 1888-1902. 5 vols. 1 ft.

For each post office the register lists names of carriers, dates of orders and effective dates of appointments, salaries, dates of promotions or other changes in status, and, in many cases, dates of oaths and dates of receipts of bond. The entries are arranged alphabetically by name of post office and thereunder by name of carrier. For a register of substitute carriers, see entry 87. See entry 89 for an index.

86. RECORD OF SALARIES OF REGULAR CARRIERS AT FIRST- AND SECOND-CLASS POST OFFICES. 1906-7. 3 vols. 6 in.

These volumes, which are numbered 25 to 27, contain the following information about each carrier in each post office: name, age, date of appointment and of any change in status, grade classification, and, if removed from position, reasons for removal. For large offices the names of substitute laborers and janitors are also given. Arranged alphabetically by name of post office and thereunder, for large offices, alphabetically by name of carrier, or, for small offices, chronologically by date of appointment.

87. REGISTER OF SUBSTITUTE CARRIERS IN FIRST- AND SECOND-CLASS POST OFFICES. 1889-1903. 2 vols. 4 in.

For each post office the register lists each substitute carrier's name, date of appointment and effective date of service, and date of his oath and date of receipt of his bond. The entries are arranged alphabetically by name of post office and thereunder by name of carrier. See entry 85 for a register of regular carriers and entry 88 for an index to part of this series.

88. INDEX TO NAMES OF SUBSTITUTE CARRIERS IN FIRST- AND SECOND-CLASS POST OFFICES. 1892-96. 1 vol. 1 in.

Listed are the carrier's name and date of appointment and a code number for the name of the post office. This index covers part of the register described in entry 87. The entries are arranged alphabetically by name of carrier.

89. INDEX TO NAMES OF CARRIERS IN SMALL CITY POST OFFICES. 1888-1902. 1 vol. 1 in.

This is an index to part of the register described in entry 85. Listed are each carrier's name, date of appointment, date of any change in status, and a code number for the name of the post office. The entries are arranged alphabetically by name of carrier.

90. ESTIMATES OF THE NUMBER OF CLERKS AND CARRIERS NEEDED BY FIRST- AND SECOND-CLASS POST OFFICES FOR THE FISCAL YEAR 1924. May-June 1923. 2 ft.

Included are work reports, recommendations for promotions, plans of working quarters, and designations of routes. Arranged alphabetically by State and thereunder by city.

91. REPORTS CONCERNING INSPECTIONS OF CITY DELIVERY SERVICE AT BALTIMORE, MD., KALAMAZOO, MICH., AND PITTSBURGH, PA. 1929-31. 2 in.

A part of a much larger series of records, most of which has been destroyed. The reports show in detail the operation of city delivery service in these cities. Arranged by city.

92. RECORDS RELATING TO THE DETROIT RIVER STEAMBOAT SERVICE. 1895-1928. 1 ft.

Under this service, inaugurated in 1895, mail was supplied to Great Lakes steamers passing through the Detroit River. The records include correspondence, contracts, blueprints, and photographs of facilities. Arranged chronologically.

RECORDS OF THE DIVISION OF RURAL DELIVERY SERVICE

93. GENERAL HEADQUARTERS CORRESPONDENCE. 1898-1936. 106 ft.

Arranged in three groups: (1) by State and thereunder by county, (2) by State and thereunder by post office, and (3) in part by a general subject grouping. The first two groups contain reports concerning the establishment, revision, and discontinuance of rural mail routes, samples of petitions for their establishment; and blueprints. The third group includes correspondence regarding the conditions of roads, cost summaries for rural free delivery service, reports of rural carriers removed, correspondence relating to motortruck routes, and statements concerning a revision of the rural mail service made in 1915. Some records relating to the Motor Vehicle Service are included for the period 1903-29.

94. RECORDS OF THE SUPERINTENDENT OF THE FREE DELIVERY SYSTEM, DIVISION OF RURAL DELIVERY. 1901-6. 2 ft.

Forms, instructions, orders, circular letters, and related records. Arranged in two groups and thereunder chronologically.

95. STATISTICAL STATEMENT OF THE FREE DELIVERY SERVICE. 1896-1910. 2 vols. 4 in.

Contains the name of each post office and the date of establishment of its free delivery service as well as an annual record of the gross receipts, cost of service, percent of cost to gross receipts, population of city, an estimate of population served by the post office, number of carriers, average number of people served by carrier, square miles served by carrier, number of letter boxes, number of business and residential deliveries, number of mounted carriers, average office time spent in a 10-day period, total time spent in a 10-day period, cost of horse hire, and cost of carfare. Arranged alphabetically by name of post office and thereunder chronologically.

RECORDS OF THE DIVISION OF POST OFFICE SERVICE

96. MISCELLANEOUS CORRESPONDENCE OF THE SUPERINTENDENT OF THE DIVISION. 1923-34. 3 in.

Copies of orders and suggestions from the First Assistant Postmaster General, mainly concerning the expeditious handling of mail and other matters under the jurisdiction of the Division.

97. REPORTS CONCERNING THE RELATIVE IMPORTANCE OF TYPES OF WORK DONE BY POSTAL CLERKS AND CARRIERS. May 1912. 2 in.

Submitted by the 100 largest post offices in response to a request from the First Assistant Postmaster General. The reports classify the type of work done in each post office. Arranged alphabetically by State and thereunder by city.

98. FORMS USED IN THE CHICAGO POST OFFICE "UNIT SYSTEM" OF WORK REPORTS. ca. 1931-34. 2 in.

Chiefly blank forms. Included are some completed summary report forms for 1932.

The forms are bound and are preceded by a list.

99. REPORTS RELATING TO OVERTIME, CHANGES IN FORCE, AND STATUS AND TYPE OF WORK. 1925-33. 3 in.
Arranged by subject and thereunder in chronological order.

100. CORRESPONDENCE AND REPORTS RELATING TO THE WEIGHING SYSTEM OF WORK MEASUREMENT. 1923-30. 4 in.
The records relate to the installation and operation, in certain large post offices, of a system of measuring the quantity of work done by weighing the amount of mail distributed. Arranged in rough chronological order.

RECORDS OF THE DIVISION OF DEAD LETTERS

101. MISCELLANEOUS RECORDS. 1897-1930. 6 in.
Included are a catalog of a Dead Letter Office sale in 1900; copies of letters relating to German claims for indemnity for mails captured in the Spanish-American War; correspondence regarding the establishment of dead letter offices in Puerto Rico, Hawaii, and the Philippines; and some general correspondence of the Division for the period 1900-30. There are also some records for the period 1867-81, including a statement of the number of letters received and returned at the Dead Letter Office in the period 1870-81, and statistics concerning the proportion of advertised dead letters delivered at the Office in July 1867.

RECORDS OF THE BUREAU OF THE SECOND ASSISTANT POSTMASTER GENERAL

RECORDS OF THE IMMEDIATE OFFICE OF THE SECOND ASSISTANT POSTMASTER GENERAL

The immediate office of the Second Assistant Postmaster General was responsible for all administrative matters of the Bureau involving relations with other Government agencies. The Second Assistant Postmaster General and his deputies represented the Department in matters under their jurisdiction, coordinated and supervised the activities of the Bureau, interpreted its policies, and approved the certifications submitted by other Bureau officials to the Comptroller General to obtain payment for services and for personnel.

102. LETTERS SENT. 1891-1934. 10 ft.
In three chronological groups: (1) press copies of instructions, 1891-1904, to special agents of the Railway Mail Service, relating to complaints against the postal service (5 vols.); (2) press copies of letters, 1903-15, concerning the administration and operation of the Bureau of the Second Assistant Postmaster General (33 vols.); and (3) reading files, 1921-34, of E. H. Shaughnessy, Paul Henderson, W. Irving Glover, and W. W. Howes, who were successively Second Assistant Postmasters General.

103. MISCELLANEOUS LETTERS SENT. 1908-33. 2 ft.
Relate to economies effected, 1908-19; issuance of postal laws and regulations; the Postal Savings System; the postal service in France; censorship of foreign mails, 1917-18; "star" mail routes (see page 20); inventions; transportation of gold coin; and personnel. One part of the series, labeled "Special Files, II-XVI," consists of copies of outgoing correspondence, 1913-16, of Joseph Stewart, Second Assistant Postmaster General, concerning pneumatic tube service in New York City, the readjustment of railway mail compensation, and improvements in railway mail service. Arranged for the most part chronologically.

104. MEMORANDA. 1914-29. 1 ft.
Relate to the railway mail service, the international postal service, and railway adjustments. A few of the memoranda relate to airmail service. Arranged chronologically.

105. CORRESPONDENCE RELATING TO AIRMAIL SERVICE. 1921-27. 2 ft.
Concerns the administration, operation, and maintenance of airmail service during the period when it was Government-owned and Government-operated. With the correspondence are copies of postal inspectors' reports made in 1925 relating to airmail service during the period 1921-24. Arranged chronologically.

106. NOTICES TO RAILWAY COMPANIES. Feb. 10, 1885-May 19, 1909. 40 vols. 7 ft.
Mainly press copies of notification and circulars (Forms 2501, 2505, 2508, 2509, 2510, 2511, 2514, 2516, 2519, 2522, 2523, 2526, and 2527) issued to railway companies. The records relate

to pay adjustments, laws concerning pay for the transportation of mails on railroad routes, the establishment and discontinuance of post offices and mail services, changes in names and sites of post offices, mail messenger services, and the weighing of mail. Arranged chronologically.

107. ANNUAL REPORTS OF THE SECOND ASSISTANT POSTMASTER GENERAL. 1911-31. 10 in.

Manuscript copies of the reports, with some related correspondence. The records are incomplete for the period 1920-31. Arranged chronologically.

108. MONTHLY REPORTS OF CHANGES. 1922-30. 2 in.

Describe new operations or improvements in airmail, railway mail, and international postal services. The reports also contain discussions of the effect of new legislation on the services. Arranged chronologically.

109. REPORTS OF STAFF CONFERENCES. 1921-23. 1 in.

An incomplete series of reports concerning conferences at which were discussed such topics as mail contracts, foreign mail service, terminal mail service, appropriations, the Universal Postal Union, sea post, personnel problems, airmail service, Cuban mail service, budget allotments, and railway mail service. Each report includes a list of representatives of the various postal services who attended that conference. The reports are arranged chronologically. Only Nos. 8, 10-34, and 37-62 are included.

110. ROSTER OF BUREAU EMPLOYEES. Nov. 1893-Jan. 1912. 1 vol. 1 in.

Shows the State from which each employee was appointed, date of entering employment and salary at that time, dates of promotions, and the division in which he was employed. Arranged chronologically, thereunder by position classification, and thereunder alphabetically by name of employee.

RECORDS OF THE
SPECIAL ADMINISTRATIVE AIDE

From about 1920 to 1946 a special administrative aide to the Second Assistant Postmaster General acted as budgetary control and personnel officer for the Bureau. He was concerned mainly with the preparation and justification of the Bureau's budget and with the distribution of appropriation allotments to the Bureau.

111. BUDGET ESTIMATES AND REPORTS ON APPROPRIATIONS. July 1920-June 1933. 4 ft.

Estimates from each division and service of the Bureau, together with reports on the apportionment of appropriations. Also included are some reports and correspondence relating to deficiency appropriations, 1920-30, and some statements of balances, 1928-29. Arranged by type of report and thereunder chronologically by fiscal year.

112. PERSONNEL RECORDS. 1918-33. 2 ft.

Monthly statistical reports of personnel changes in the field services, 1921-32; statistics concerning salaries and related correspondence on personnel changes, 1920-33; miscellaneous memoranda relating to personnel actions, the dispatching of mail, and arrangements for women to live in Government-operated hotels, 1918-20; weekly work-progress reports from all divisions, January 4, 1926-December 26, 1933; and monthly overtime reports, 1925-33. Arranged by type of record as listed and thereunder chronologically.

RECORDS OF THE DIVISION
OF RAILWAY MAIL SERVICE

Mail was first carried by railway in 1831, when a mail contractor utilized the services of the South Carolina Railroad. On December 5, 1832, the Post Office Department recognized this mode of transportation by permitting mail contractors to use railroad transportation from Lancaster to West Chester, Pa.; and on July 7, 1838, an act of Congress (5 Stat. 283) declared all railroads in the United States to be post routes. Service by railroad thereafter increased rapidly. In many cases, contractors for "star" routes were permitted to use the railroads in the performance of their contracts; in other cases, contracts were made directly with the railroad companies.

The first record of a clerk's appointment to have charge of the mails on a railroad run is for John E. Kendall's appointment in May 1837. On June 19, 1837, John Elliott was appointed as railroad mail agent; and, on February 3, 1838, John Mitchell was notified of his appointment "to superintend the mails" on the railroad run from Washington to Philadelphia. In June 1840 the traveling railway post office came into being when two agents were appointed to accompany the mail from Boston to Springfield, Mass., "to make exchanges of mails, attend to delivery, and receive and forward all unpaid way letters and packages received." The railway mail clerks were supervised by the postmaster at one terminal of the run. Before 1864 mails were sorted at the large post offices, and only mail intended for delivery at local points on the line was sorted on the railroad cars.

The Railway Post Office Service was established on July 7, 1862, to facilitate the distribution of overland mail on the route from Hannibal, Mo., to St. Joseph, Mo. This service was extended to the eastern seaboard by 1864; and in that year the Office of the Superintendent of Railway Mail Service was established, with eastern and western divisions separated by the eastern boundary of the State of Indiana. The Office, which later included the Railway Post Office Service, became a part of the Bureau of the Second Assistant Postmaster General about 1873. On July 1, 1907, it became the Division of Railway Mail Service. The Division's field service consisted of 15 divisions, with a superintendent in charge of each. To simplify further the distribution of railway mail, the Division began side, terminal, and transfer services shortly before World War I.

Immediately preceding the 1946 reorganization of the Bureau of the Second Assistant Postmaster General, the Division of Railway Mail Service supervised matters relating to the establishment of any changes in railway mail service, the handling of mail in transmit, appointments of railway postal clerks, the admission of matter to the mails that would be injurious to the mails or to postal employees, the distribution to the postal service of mail pouches and sacks and mail-pouch locks, and matters relating to the star route service and the highway post office service.

113. SUBJECT INDEX TO CORRESPONDENCE OF THE GENERAL SUPERINTENDENT OF THE RAILWAY MAIL SERVICE. 1889-1915. 1 vol. 2 in.

The correspondence indexed by this volume has not been identified. The index, however, gives a brief summary of each letter. Arranged alphabetically by subject.

114. MISCELLANEOUS CORRESPONDENCE. 1902-29. 3 ft.

Relates to complaints about and suggestions for improvements in railway mail service, 1924-29; publicity concerning the service, 1918-26; side mail, closed-pouch mail, franked mail, and missent mail, 1912-25; devices for discharging mail from moving trains, 1902-6; mail protection and damage, 1919-24; use of firearms by employees of the Division, 1924-27; unsatisfactory service at the Baltimore & Ohio Railroad station

at Pittsburgh, Pa., 1917-18; employee organizations, 1918-23; and the handling of mail for mail-order houses, 1918-23. With the correspondence is a study of railway mail service in the Boston postal district, 1919-21. Arranged by subject as listed and thereunder chronologically.

115. INSTRUCTION CIRCULARS. 1921-34. 2 ft.

Sent to the field superintendents of the railway mail service. Arranged by date of circular.

116. DECISIONS AND INSTRUCTIONS RELATING TO THE HANDLING OF MAIL ON A SPACE-OCCUPIED BASIS. 1917-20. 8 in.

Relate to the change, on July 28, 1916, in the method of paying railroad companies for carrying the mail. Previously they had been paid according to the weight of the mail carried; after this date they were to be paid according to the space occupied by the mail. The records are arranged by field division of the Service.

117. MONTHLY REPORTS ON THE COSTS OF OPERATING RAILWAY POSTAL LINES. 1922-28. 4 in.

Tabulations showing field division, railway postal line, number of clerks employed on the line, their salaries (including overtime for the month), total travel allowances for and travel expenses of substitute clerks, salaries for substitute clerks instead of annual leave, total cost of mail distribution, number of mail pouches opened, number of packages and mail sacks handled, number of registers maintained by each field division, total units of mail handled, average number of units handled by each clerk, and number of units handled per $1,000 expense. The reports are arranged chronologically.

118. INDEXES TO ROSTERS OF RAILWAY POSTAL CLERKS. 1883-97. 3 vols. 7 in.

The indexes are arranged chronologically, with entries arranged alphabetically by name of clerk.

119. ROSTERS OF SPECIAL, ROUTE, AND LOCAL BLANK AND STAMP AGENTS AND ROSTERS OF RAILWAY POSTAL CLERKS. 1855-97. 24 vols. 5 ft.

The rosters of special, route, and local blank and stamp agents are dated 1855-62; the rosters of railway postal clerks, 1862-97. The rosters contain the name of the railroad, the name and date of appointment of the agent or clerk, and occasionally the date of taking the oath. Up to 1883, the volumes contain alphabetical indexes by name of person, route, or railroad; from 1883 on, the indexes are in separate volumes (see entry 118). The rosters are arranged chronologically.

120. NEWSLETTERS. 1918-51. 23 ft.

Weekly newsletters from the 15 division superintendents to the General Superintendent of the Railway Mail Service. The newsletters relate to holiday mail, Presidential mail, cargo mail, train schedules, storage-car movements, terminal facilities, accidents, summer service, labor complaints, postage rates, cost of mail distribution, merchandise handled, parcel post, weather reports, steamship mail, meetings of the superintendents, personnel, the Railway Mail Association, mail service in Alaska, daylight saving time, airmail, service interruptions, locks and empty equipment, star route service, postmasters' conventions, registered mail, inspections, effects of the depression on the service, bonus payments to employees, and statistics regarding mail handling. Arranged by date of issuance.

121. DAILY SCHEDULES OF MAIL TRAINS. 1882-84. 3 vols. 5 in.

These printed schedules serve as a concise record of authorized mail route operations by the Railway Mail Service. They contain information on the schedules of closed-pouch mail trains, foreign mails, and steamboat service. At the beginning of each schedule there is a description of the work performed by the division of the Railway Mail Service affected by the schedule. Arranged by volume number, I-III, and thereunder by field division number, 1-15.

122. REGISTERS OF RAILROAD MAIL-ROUTE CONTRACTS. 1877-1948. 658 vols. 138 ft.

The backstrip of each volume shows the contract years and the States covered. For each contract are given the mail-route number (with changes, if any), terminals of the route and intervening post office stops, distances between railway stations, time schedule for the route, name and address of contractor for the route, date of contract award, amount of contract bid, and any contract changes. The contract changes refer to increases or decreases in contract payments, changes in schedules, changes in routes, or changes in subcontractors. The registers contain references to transportation of mail by steamboat, city railway, and suburban electric line. Occasionally the registers give the dates of

establishment and discontinuance of post offices, post office name changes, names of competitive bidders for the mail-route contract and the amounts of their bids, and descriptions of mail routes on branch railway lines. The volumes are arranged chronologically by 4-year contract period and thereunder by State within the contract section.

RECORDS RELATING TO THE STAR ROUTE SERVICE

In 1775, to replace the postal service operated by the British, the Continental Congress established a system of posts for carrying letters and intelligence. As the country developed, the number of post offices increased and more post roads were constructed. The use of railroads as a means of transporting mail increased rapidly after 1838, and the use of post riders and horse-drawn vehicles for carrying the mail was limited to post offices that were not on the railroad mail routes. An act of March 3, 1845, contained the provision in which the modern star route originated, namely, that the Postmaster General was to award contracts for mail transportation "to the lowest bidder, tendering sufficient guarantees for faithful performance, without other reference to the mode of such transportation than may be necessary to provide for the due celerity, certainty, and security of such transportation . . . . " The practice of marking with three stars (or asterisks) many of the contracts for mail service providing "due celerity, certainty, and security" developed; and eventually the transportation of mail between post offices by all modes except boat and railway became known as star route mail service, which was operated by the Railway Mail Service. These star routes were intended to serve small post offices located off the lines of railroad travel and those families who live between the post offices.

When rural free delivery service began in 1896, wherever it was found feasible for rural service to supersede star route service the contracts for the latter were abrogated. Occasionally star route service was reestablished when the rural service was no longer needed. On October 1, 1910, star route service, excepting that in Alaska, was consolidated with rural free delivery service within the Division of Rural Mails, Bureau of the Fourth Assistant Postmaster General, in order that all questions relating to rural mail service could be decided in one office. On July 8, 1929, the service was transferred back to the Bureau of the Second Assistant, where it was supervised by the Division of Railway Mail Service until 1946.

123. LETTERS SENT. Sept. 1862-Apr. 1863.
1 vol. 6 in.
Arranged chronologically.

124. INDEXES TO REGISTERS FOR STAR ROUTE CONTRACTS. 1830-74, 1883-87, 1901-60. 68 vols. and unbound papers. 51 ft.

The backstrip of each volume shows the contract years and the States covered. Each volume contains an alphabetical list of post offices connected by star routes, with the county and State in which each post office is located and the mail-route number or numbers of the post office. In some cases the index shows name changes of post offices; dates of establishment, discontinuance, and reopening of post offices after the Civil War; whether post offices were privately maintained or located on special routes; and the annual cost of certain mail route services. Volumes marked "1855-1859 Virginia," "1855-1859 Georgia, " and "1855-1860 Ohio" also give the terminal points of the routes. Some of the registers are described in entry 125. The volumes are arranged chronologically by contract term and thereunder geographically by State. For the period 1903-60 the records are on 3" x 5" cards.

125. REGISTERS FOR STAR ROUTE CONTRACTS. 1814-1960. 622 vols. and unbound papers. 228 ft.

(1) Volumes (622) for the years 1814-17, 1824, and 1828-1935. The backstrip of each volume shows the contract years and the States covered. For the purpose of issuing advertisements for bids and contracting for transportation of mails on star routes, the United States was divided into four contract sections; new contracts for terms of 4 years were made in some of the sections each year. For each contract are usually given the mail-route number (with changes, if any), terminals of the route and the intervening post office stops, the county and State where each post office on the route is located, other mail-route numbers of each post office, distance between each post office on the route, time schedule for the route, name and address of contractor for the route, date of awarding contract, amount of contract bid, mode to be used in transporting the mail, and any contract changes (increase or decrease of contract payments, changes in schedule or route, or changes in subcontractors).

In a few cases the registers give the dates of establishment, discontinuance, and reestablishment of post offices; post office name changes; names of competitive bidders for contracts and the amounts of their bids; and information concerning special routes to post offices off the main mail route, routes by way of the Great Lakes or rivers, the Overland Route, routes to countries bordering the Gulf of Mexico, and routes to Canada, Cuba, Great Britain, islands in the Pacific, and the Orient. Some of the volumes contain Post Office Department circulars; miscellaneous orders (appointments of mail messengers and local agents, printing instructions, and advertisements); and post office receipts. The volumes are arranged chronologically by contract term and within each volume the entries are arranged for the most part by State. Indexes to some of the volumes are described in entry 124.

(2) Forms 4134 (green) and 5-5415 (white), for the years 1914-60. Form 4134--an announcement advertising for bids--shows the State, county, mail-route number, a description of the mail route, amount of bond to be posted, mileage for the route, number of round trips to be made per week, time schedule for the route, names of bidders and the amounts of their bids, name of the successful bidder, and, occasionally, information about readvertising for bids and about the mail route, including names of post offices along the route. Form 5-5415--the order of the Postmaster General for the contract--gives the number and date of the order, terminals of the mail route, length of the route, number of round trips to be made per week, time schedule for the route, name of the contractor, and, occasionally, date of contract changes. For the period 1930-60 the registers relate only to Alaska and Hawaii. The forms, which are interfiled, are arranged chronologically by contract period and thereunder alphabetically by State. See also entries 130-132.

126. LISTS OF STAR ROUTE MAIL CONTRACTORS. 1833-77. 36 vols. 5 ft.

The backstrip of each volume shows the contract years and the names of the States for which contractors are listed. Within each volume are the names of the contractors, their addresses, and the numbers of the routes they serviced. The volume entitled 1861 Ante-Bellum Mail Service also lists the terminal points of the route, deductions, fines assessed, and dates of certificate issuances. Some of the volumes contain information relating to cancellations or transfers of contracts, to route terminals, and to the annual cost of specific route service. In general the volumes are arranged chronologically by contract term. Within each volume the listings are arranged by State and thereunder alphabetically by name of contractor. In volumes containing names for more than one contract section the arrangement is by section, thereunder by State, and thereunder alphabetically by name of contractor.

127. PAY BOOKS FOR STAR SERVICE. 1851-66. 52 vols. 10 ft.
Arranged chronologically.

128. REGISTER OF RECEIPT WARRANTS. 1836-1942. 2 vols. 4 in.
Arranged chronologically.

RECORDS RELATING TO STAR SERVICE
BY MOTORTRUCKS

Section 7 of an act of July 2, 1918, appropriated funds for conducting experiments in the operation of motor-vehicle truck routes in rural communities "to promote the conservation of farm products and to facilitate the collection and delivery thereof from producer to consumer, and the delivery of articles necessary in the production of such food products to the producers . . . ." In 1920 the experiment was abandoned as impracticable, but the existing routes were continued for several years.

129. RECORDS OF GOVERNMENT-OPERATED STAR SERVICE BY MOTORTRUCKS. 1917-24. 26 ft.
In six groups as follows: (1) general correspondence, 1917-24, relating (a) to the purchase, maintenance, and repair of equipment, arranged by subject in arbitrarily numbered classifications assigned apparently in consecutive order as the need arose; (b) to the operation, management, maintenance, and equipment of motortruck service on star routes, arranged by star route number; and (c) to orders establishing, extending, and discontinuing routes for star service by motortrucks, arranged chronologically; (2) correspondence relating to the establishment of motortruck service on star routes, 1917-19; (3) correspondence, 1919-20, relating to farm-product deliveries within the Washington, D. C., area and in Virginia, West Virginia, Maryland, Pennsylvania, and Delaware; (4) monthly accounts for expenditures and operating costs, 1918-22; (5) statements of mail handled, 1919-20; and (6) office files of C. T. Butler, superintendent for Pennsylvania, relating to the maintenance of the garage, equipment, and

supplies at Oxford, Pa., 1921-22. The records in groups 2-6 are arranged chronologically within each group.

130. RECORDS RELATING TO THE ESTABLISHMENT OF HIGHWAY POST OFFICES. 1940-59. 4 ft.
Case files relating to the establishment of highway-post-office routes, 1940-59. They include reports, correspondence, maps, and other records relating to the authorization of the routes and the initiation of service. Arranged chronologically.

RECORDS RELATING TO
POWERBOAT SERVICE

This service, established in 1841, provided for delivery of mail on a contract basis to post offices located on inland rivers, lakes, and bays of the continental United States, Alaska, Hawaii, and Puerto Rico; and to points between the United States and the Territory of Alaska. Initial requests for powerboat service came from the First Assistant Postmaster General, in connection with the establishment of post offices or when residents of an area petitioned for service. Service was established upon recommendation of the divisional superintendents of the Railway Mail Service, if inspection indicated that such service was necessary.

131. REGISTERS OF ORDERS CONCERNING POWERBOAT- AND STEAMBOAT-MAIL-ROUTE SERVICE. 1859-63; July 1, 1910-June 30, 1947. 14 vols. and unbound papers. 7 ft.
The registers contain the original signed and approved orders authorizing the establishment, change, or discontinuance of powerboat or steamboat routes in the 4th Contract Section (Arkansas, Louisiana, Texas, Idaho, Washington, Oregon, California, Hawaii, and Alaska) of the United States. The orders show the names of the contractor and vessel, stopping places along the route, terminals, mileage between stops, total mileage, rate of pay per mile, and total amount paid for the contract. For the period 1914-47 the orders relate only to Alaska and Hawaii. For the period 1859-63 they relate only to South Carolina, California, Utah, and Nevada. The orders are arranged consecutively by mail-route number.

132. POWERBOAT MAIL SERVICE CONTRACTS IN THE UNITED STATES AND HAWAII. 1949-53. 6 in.
Arranged alphabetically by State or Territory.

133. RECORDS RELATING TO POWERBOAT MAIL SERVICE IN VIRGINIA. 1921-25. 8 in.

Relate to mail-route contract cases that were later adjusted by the Division of Railway Adjustments. The case folders contain advertisements, bids, orders relating to contract changes, petitions for mail service, sureties of mail contractors, subcontracts, maps, and general correspondence about each mail route. Arranged by mail-route contract number, 14082 to 14100.

134. GENERAL CORRESPONDENCE. 1858-1916, 1942-52. 7 ft.

The records are fragmentary. Some of the material refers to Alaska. The records are arranged chronologically.

RECORDS OF THE DIVISION OF RAILWAY ADJUSTMENTS

An act of July 7, 1838, fixed the rate of compensation for transportation of mail by railroads at not more than 25 percent over and above the cost of similar transportation by post coaches. On January 25, 1839, the rate of compensation was increased and on February 20, 1845, the Postmaster General was authorized by a joint congressional resolution to enter into contracts with railroad companies without advertising bids. In May of that year he was directed to divide the railroad routes into three classes.

These laws remained in force until an act of March 3, 1873, established a scale of rates based on the daily average weight of the mail carried and provided that on each railroad route the mails be weighed for a period of 30 days and not less frequently than once in 4 years. In 1878 the Division of Railway Adjustments was created to handle arrangements in establishing rates for new railroad routes and to make adjustments in existing mail service on steam and electric railways, steam vessels, and some star routes, and in airmail service in Alaska and the mail messenger service. The Division audited claims for such types of mail transportation, examined quality of performance, prepared statements of accounts for payment of the various carriers, and, after 1916, interpreted and applied the regulations and orders of the Interstate Commerce Commission and the Civil Aeronautics Board.

In 1916 the act of 1873 was amended to provide that payments to railroad companies for carrying the mail be based on the size of the railway post-office car rather than on the weight of the mail carried. The amending act also specified maximum rates of payment and directed the Interstate Commerce Commission to determine and maintain fair and reasonable rates of payment.

135. GENERAL CORRESPONDENCE. 1907-46. 20 ft.

Mainly correspondence relating to administration, operations, personnel, rulings, and instructions of and appropriations for the Division, with references to the Alaska star route, Alaska airmail, and powerboat, electric car, and side messenger mail services. Included are correspondence with railroad companies relating to backpay due as a result of an Interstate Commerce Commission order of July 10, 1928, and to equalization deduction cases; reports on amounts of fines paid by the railroad companies; reports on tests in the use of narrow-gage railroad units; reports on costs of mail transportation; work papers for a pamphlet containing instructions and rulings on transportation of mails by railroads; and weekly progress reports on expenditures for space authorizations and railroad transportation. Arranged in part by subject.

136. CASE FILES AND GENERAL CORRESPONDENCE RELATING TO PRIVATE EXPRESS. 1896-1933. 11 ft.

Relate to the transmittal of monthly bills, statements, letters, and packages by means other than the postal service that were in violation of Federal statutes. Correspondence for the period 1932-33 is arranged alphabetically by name of State; case files for the period 1896-1932 are arranged by case number, and those for the period 1932-33 are arranged alphabetically by name of violator.

137. PUBLIC CARRIERS' REPORTS OF RAILWAY MAIL SERVICE PERFORMED. 1916-22. 1 ft.

These case reports, made by the railroad companies, show name of the company, route number, period covered by the report, points of service, distance traveled, class of service provided, number of one-way trips, and rate per mile. Included are some Department affidavits approving railroad company statements and correspondence regarding adjustments in increased rates. Arranged numerically by report case number, 107501 to 107516 and 103503 to 103514.

138. REPORTS RELATING TO EQUALIZATION OF PAY BETWEEN COMPETITIVE RAILROAD MAIL ROUTES. 1911-26. 5 in.

Filed with the reports are railroad weight circulars and correspondence relating to mail schedules, weight of mail, and cost of transportation of mail in connection with 4-year contracts. Arranged chronologically.

RECORDS RELATING TO MAIL MESSENGER SERVICE

Mail messenger service between railway stations and post offices was first mentioned in the appropriation act for the fiscal year ending June 30, 1869. Until June 30, 1871, mail messengers were paid from the appropriation for inland transportation; after that date a separate appropriation was made for them. An act of March 3, 1887, enlarged the scope of the service by authorizing such mail messenger service as was necessary for carrying the mail in connection with railroad and steamboat service and with transfer service between depots, over bridges or ferries, between post offices, and between post offices and branch offices or stations in cases where the carriers were not legally required to deliver the mail they carried from or to the post offices. Beginning in 1910 this messenger service was supervised by the Division of Miscellaneous Transportation. Supervision was transferred to the Bureau of the First Assistant Postmaster General on July 1, 1916; but in the early 1920's it was returned to the Bureau of the Second Assistant, under the Division of Railway Adjustments.

139. REGISTERS OF MAIL MESSENGERS. 1877-81, 1900-47. 363 vols. 125 ft.

One volume, relating only to Rhode Island and Connecticut mail messenger routes for the contract period 1877-81, gives length of each mail route; frequency of service; messenger's name, appointment date, and salary; and date the mail route was established. Each of the other volumes contains both a statement of and a service order for individual mail messenger services during 4-year contract periods in specified States. The statement gives mail-route number, a description of the route, length of the route, name of the mail messenger, his service record, and his annual salary. The service order gives similar information, together with the date of the order. There are revised orders to cover changes in services. In some instances the dates on which messenger service was discontinued are given. The volumes are arranged chronologically by contract term and thereunder by State or States within a contract region. Within each volume the material is arranged alphabetically by name of post office to which the messenger was assigned.

140. CORRESPONDENCE RELATING TO TRANSFERS TO SIDE TERMINALS. 1927-34. 2 vols. 2 in.

Arranged by name of post office and thereunder chronologically.

RECORDS OF THE DIVISION OF INTERNATIONAL POSTAL SERVICE

The work relating to the exchange of mails with foreign countries was at first performed in the Office of the Postmaster General. As early as 1792 the Postmaster General negotiated a postal arrangement with the Deputy Postmaster General of Canada, and the postal act of 1825 authorized him to make arrangements with postmasters in foreign countries for the reciprocal receipt and delivery of mail. In 1844 Congress recognized the postal agreements with foreign postal administrations. The first postal treaty entered into by the United States was with Bremen in 1847; in 1849 one was negotiated with Great Britain.

By 1850 the work relating to the exchange of mails with foreign countries was of such importance that Horatio King was placed in charge of a separate "foreign desk" under supervision of the Office of the Postmaster General. In 1857 the supervision of the international postal service was assigned to the Bureau of the First Assistant Postmaster General. An act of July 27, 1868, authorized the Postmaster General to appoint a Superintendent of Foreign Mails and three additional clerks. According to the postal laws and regulations of 1879, the "Office of the Superintendent of Foreign Mails" was a separate division responsible directly to the Postmaster General, but on July 20, 1891, the Postmaster General ordered that the Division of Foreign Mails be assigned to the Bureau of the Second Assistant Postmaster. It was known as the Division of International Postal Service from July 7, 1928, to July 1946.

The Division was charged mainly with the management of foreign surface mail and airmail, cooperation with the Treasury Department in the clearing of mail through the customs, adjustment of indemnity claims in connection with international mails, administrative determination of amounts due from or to foreign countries, translation of foreign-language letters and documents pertaining to the international postal service, the supervision of the Navy mail service, and the handling of matters involving negotiation, conclusion, and interpretation of postal conventions and agreements (except those concerning money orders).

The Postmaster General was the custodian of most original conventions and the greater part of these are now in the National Archives (see entry 141). From February 20, 1792, to June 8, 1872, postal conventions and agreements were made under special statutes. An act passed on the latter date gave the Postmaster General authority to negotiate and conclude postal treaties or conventions by and with the advice and consent of the President. Such agreements are not submitted to the Senate but are approved and ratified by the President. Bilateral conventions are generally signed by the Postmaster General; multilateral conventions are agreed on at international postal congresses and signed by the U.S. delegates.

Five postal conventions are exceptions to the above procedure. Negotiated under the ordinary procedure of treatymaking, they are in Record Group 11, United States Government Documents Having General Legal Effect. They were concluded with New Granada, March 6, 1844 (Treaty Series 53); Great Britain, December 15, 1848 (Treaty Series 121); Mexico, December 11, 1861 (Treaty Series 211); Mexico, July 31, 1861 (Treaty Series 210--although unperfected, it was erroneously filed in the perfected series and assigned a number); and Costa Rica, June 9, 1862 (Unperfected Treaty Series 0). In the same record group there are a proposed postal convention with France, 1852; the original of a postal convention with Belgium of December 21, 1859 (Treaty Series 21); a copy of the additional convention with Italy of August 9 and 24, 1880; and a certified copy of a multilateral convention signed at the Universal Postal Congress held in Washington, D.C., in 1897. The last three treaties were not submitted to the Senate. There is also a ratified copy of the Universal Postal Convention of August 28, 1924, which was furnished to the State Department by the Post Office Department and was assigned number 708-A in the Treaty Series. An unperfected convention with Mexico of February 10, 1857 (Unperfected Treaty Series B-11), is in the series of diplomatic despatches from Mexico, in Record Group 59, General Records of the Department of State. It is possible that other conventions are in this record group among the diplomatic despatches from other countries or in Record Group 84, Records of the Foreign Service Posts of the Department of State.

Foreign parcel post was inaugurated by a convention with Jamaica, British West Indies, on October 1, 1887, and by 1891 there were 11 parcel post conventions. By September 1, 1932, there were 61 bilateral postal conventions or agreements and 1 multilateral agreement.

Complicated rates of postage and varying terms of the separate treaties with foreign countries inspired a movement to form a universal postal union, and the first international postal congress was held at Berne in 1874. The Universal Postal Union (at first called the General Postal Union) was formed as a result of the Berne congress; it met at Paris in 1878, Lisbon in 1885, Vienna in 1891, Washington in 1897, Rome in 1906, Madrid in 1920, Stockholm in 1924, London in 1929, Cairo in 1934, and Buenos Aires in 1939. Conventions of this Postal Union permit members to enter into restricted postal unions, of which the Postal Union of the Americas and Spain (signatories to which are the 21 American Republics, Canada, and Spain) is perhaps the most important.

The First South American Postal Congress, held at Montevideo in 1911, formed the South American Postal Union, which operated so successfully that other American countries expressed a wish to join. At the First Pan American Postal Congress at Buenos Aires in 1921, the South American Postal Union was transformed into the Pan American Postal Union; and at the Third Pan American Postal Congress at Madrid in 1931, the name was changed to the Postal Union of the Americas and Spain. Other congresses of these Unions were held at Mexico City in 1926, at Panama in 1936, and at Rio de Janiero in 1946.

141. RECORD COPIES OF POSTAL CONVENTIONS WITH FOREIGN COUNTRIES. 1857-1929. 3 ft.

These handwritten or typed texts of postal conventions, signed by the Postmaster General and by representatives of the foreign country concerned, are considered the U.S. record copies. The conventions with each country, together with related materials, are in separate envelopes that are arranged alphabetically by name of country. For a list of these conventions, prepared from the Post Office Department's Catalog of Postal Conventions and Agreements, see appendix III.

142. MISCELLANEOUS RECORDS RELATING TO POSTAL CONGRESSES AND CONVENTIONS. 1916-27. 8 in.

Correspondence concerning acknowledgments of postal reports from Latin American countries, steamship reservations and schedules for delegates assigned to conventions, franking privileges extended to diplomatic and consular officers, ratification of postal conventions and agreements, parcel post, and plans for postal congresses; a brief history of the General Postal Union; the articles of the Pan American Postal

Union; the agenda for the congress at Madrid (1920) and the First South American Continental Postal Congress at Montevideo (1911); postal announcements issued by Latin American countries; and newspaper clippings. Arranged in the groups listed.

RECORDS RELATING TO OCEAN MAIL SERVICE

In 1845 Congress gave the Postmaster General authority to enter into contracts for carrying foreign mail. Before that time the Postmaster General made arrangements with foreign postal administrations and with shipowners for the transportation of overseas mail.

On March 3, 1891, "An Act to provide for ocean mail service between the United States and foreign ports and to promote commerce" was approved. It authorized the Postmaster General to enter into contracts with American citizens for the carrying of mail on American steamships. Thereafter the Post Office Department contracted for sufficient shipping and space to care for its needs in handling overseas mails on several ocean-mail routes.

Under the Merchant Marine Acts of 1920 and 1928 the authority of the Postmaster General to contract for ocean mail service was continued, but with the additional provisions that it be done to aid in the development of a U.S. merchant marine and in the expansion of foreign and coastwise trade in ships under the U.S. flag. These acts were superseded by the Merchant Marine Act of 1936, which transferred the powers and duties vested in the Postmaster General with regard to ocean-mail contracts to the Maritime Commission and provided that all mail of the United States should insofar as practicable be carried on vessels of U.S. registry.

143. CORRESPONDENCE AND REPORTS CONCERNING SPEED TESTS OF CONTRACTED VESSELS. 1929-39. 4 ft.

Relate mainly to the activities of the Post Office Department that resulted from the Merchant Marine Act of 1928: testing speed capabilities of contract vessels, periodically examining the deck and engineroom logs of all vessels, and becoming familiar with physical conditions of the vessels through the study of the technical reports, surveys, and repair specifications prepared for each vessel that carried mail. Arranged by ocean-mail route number. A small amount of correspondence with the Munson Steamship Line regarding a bid for an ocean-mail contract in 1929 is filed separately.

144. QUESTIONNAIRES RELATING TO OCEAN-MAIL ROUTES. 1933-34. 1 ft.

These were answered by American steamship owners and operators in foreign countries. The questionnaires contain information relating to vessels, their comparative capacities, subventions, trade routes, competitive conditions in carrying the mail, and operations.

RECORDS RELATING TO FOREIGN AND MILITARY POSTAL SERVICE

The Spanish-American War made it necessary to establish a military postal service to handle mail for 250,000 soldiers. The first military post office was set up at Camp Black, N.Y., on May 4, 1898, and was given all the powers of a regular post office. As other offices were established and the volume of business increased, trained postal clerks were assigned to the military post offices throughout the United States.

As the military forces advanced into Cuba, Puerto Rico, and the Philippine Islands, postal services that were closely associated with the general postal system of the United States were established on these islands. The post offices in Cuba and Puerto Rico were supervised by the Railway Mail Service; and those on the Philippine Islands, by the San Francisco Superintendent of Delivery. In 1899 the United States set up a postal system in Cuba similar to its own and on May 20, 1902, relinquished most of its control to the Cuban Government. Some details of U.S. administration were not settled until 1908.

145. ADMINISTRATIVE CORRESPONDENCE RELATING TO MILITARY POSTAL SERVICE. 1898-1902. 8 in.

Relates to personnel, equipment, and supplies for military postal stations in the Hawaiian and Philippine Islands, China, Puerto Rico, Cuba, and the States of Alabama, Florida, Georgia, Kentucky, New York, Tennessee, and Virginia. Arranged by subject as listed.

146. RECORDS RELATING TO THE CUBAN POSTAL SERVICE. 1896-1908. 6 ft.

Correspondence of the Post Office Department, Congress, the Military Governor of Cuba, the Cuban Collector of Customs, the Cuban Treasurer, and Cuban postmasters relating to the operation and administration of the Cuban postal service; office files of Estes G. Rathbone, Director General of Cuban Posts; letters of application and recommendation; a list of postal employees; photographs of employees; a report for the period January 1-May 20, 1902; confidential reports relating to Cuban reaction to U.S. military occupation; newspaper clippings; orders of administration and operation issued by the Director General of Cuban Posts; forms; and indexes to correspondence. The correspondence is arranged by subject; the other records are grouped by type as listed.

147. RECORDS RELATING TO THE PHILIPPINE ISLANDS POSTAL SERVICE. 1895-1903. 1 ft.

Mainly correspondence and memoranda of the Post Office Department and Congress relating to the operations and administration of the Philippine postal service; case files for claims of special employees; lists of postal employees; photographs of employees; letters of application and recommendation; vouchers and receipts for postal equipment; statements of receipts and expenditures for the period 1889-1901; and reports of mail, parcels, and money orders received and dispatched for the United States and foreign countries. Included is some correspondence relating to the establishment of a postal system at Camp Merritt, San Francisco, Calif. Arranged chronologically.

148. RECORDS RELATING TO THE PUERTO RICAN POSTAL SERVICE. 1899-1900. 1 in.

Included are reports to the Post Office Department containing lists of postal employees in Puerto Rico; an inventory of supplies and equipment; statements of stamps received and sold; and accounts of receipts and disbursements. Arranged in the groups listed.

RECORDS RELATING TO THE
FOREIGN AIRMAIL SERVICE

The first airmail route from the United States to another country was inaugurated on October 15, 1920, from Seattle, Wash., to Victoria, British Columbia, to connect with steamships to and from the Orient. On November 1, 1920, an airmail route was established between Key West, Fla., and Havana, Cuba. This route was discontinued in 1923 but was reestablished on October 19, 1927, the date that marks the beginning of foreign airmail service as it is known today. Impetus to the expansion of foreign airmail routes was furnished by an act approved March 8, 1928, authorizing the Postmaster General to enter into contracts for not more than 10-year periods for the transportation of mail by air to foreign countries and to insular possessions of the United States.

149. CORRESPONDENCE RELATING TO AIRMAIL SERVICE. 1918-29, 1934-37. 8 in.

Contains complaints, inquiries, and suggestions concerning airmail service. Correspondence for the period 1918-29 is that of the Division of Foreign Mails; the later correspondence relates to the transpacific airmail service. Arranged chronologically.

150. SCHEDULES FOR AIRLINES. 1928-36. 20 ft.

Included is some related correspondence. Arranged for the most part chronologically.

151. RECORDS CONCERNING AIRMAIL SERVICE TO CENTRAL AMERICA. 1924-26. 3 in.

Included are correspondence with the Department of State concerning surveys and reports on and reactions to airmail service with countries of Central America; petitions and reports of the New Orleans Association of Commerce favoring the establishment of such an airmail service; and Army surveys of flight routes.

152. REPORTS OF PAN AMERICAN AIRWAYS AND OF FOREIGN AIRMAIL CARRIERS. 1934-37. 2 ft.

Financial statements and operating reports collected by the Special Audit Section of the Division of International Postal Service for the purpose of comparing foreign and domestic airmail rates. The records relating to Pan American Airways include the following: Form FAM 5-10 (miles, frequency, and rates); Form FAM-10 (average and minimum flying time between points); Schedule No. 2 (direct aircraft operating expenses); a report on property investments of Pan American Airways; an analysis of disbursements to accounts concerning the Caribbean division; and statistics on costs, flight routes, pilots' salaries, depreciation, passengers and revenues, mail express, and excess baggage. The records pertaining to foreign airmail carriers show passenger income, divisional (operating) expenses, airport expenses, and costs (present values and depreciations). The records are arranged for the most part chronologically and thereunder by airline company.

153. PERFORMANCE REPORTS ON FOREIGN AIRMAIL SERVICE. 1938-39. 5 in.

Monthly reports (Form 2718) showing route number, a description of the route, number of scheduled trips, number of trips arriving at end of route, causes of delays, and performance records (canceled and partially completed trips, and miles flown). Arranged chronologically.

RECORDS OF THE DIVISION OF AIR MAIL SERVICE

The development of domestic airmail service began with special or exhibition flights made by permission of the Post Office Department-- without expense to the Department--on the occasion of State fairs or local celebrations. During the week of September 27-30, 1911, mail was dropped in pouches at Mineola, N.Y., for the postmaster to pick up. After that the Post Office Department granted permission for mail to be carried on short exhibition and experimental flights between certain points. During the fiscal year 1916 funds for airmail service were made available from the appropriation for steamboat or other powerboat service; and, on June 30, 1918, Congress appropriated $100,000 for experimental airmail routes. From November 15, 1918, to February 15, 1919, all airmail service was owned and operated directly by the Government. On the latter date, airmail service routes between Detroit and Chicago and between Detroit and Cleveland were let to private contractors. After September 1, 1927, all airmail service routes were let to private contractors, and the Government ceased actual operation of the airmail service except for a short period in the early 1930's.

With the exception of the period August 8, 1938-July 2, 1940, when the Division of Air Mail Service was administered and supervised by the Bureau of the First Assistant Postmaster General, the Division was operated as a field service under the supervision of the Second Assistant Postmaster General. On July 1, 1944, it was transferred to the departmental service within the Bureau of the Second Assistant Postmaster General.

154. CORRESPONDENCE RELATING TO THE OPERATION OF AUTOGIRO AND HELICOPTER MAIL, AND THE FIRST AIRMAIL FREIGHT MAIL IN THE UNITED STATES AND ALASKA. 1919-35. 10 ft.
Included are general reports and schedules. Arranged chronologically.

155. RECORDS RELATING TO PROPOSED AND REQUESTED AIRMAIL AND HELICOPTER ROUTES AND STOPS. 1926-49. 12 ft.
Included are correspondence, petitions, photographs, maps, blueprints, brochures published by cities, and surveys. Arranged by name of city

156. CASE FILES OF HEARINGS ON ESTABLISHING POSTAL HELICOPTER SERVICE. 1928-40. 6 ft.
Included are exhibits and photographs. The records are arranged by State and thereunder chronologically.

157. GENERAL RECORDS OF THE AIRMAIL SERVICE AND ITS SUCCESSORS. 1918-42. 95 ft.
Correspondence, reports, and memoranda, in three groups: (1) records of the airmail service, 1918-25, (2) records of the General Superintendent of the Airmail Service, 1926-42, and (3) records of the Second Assistant Postmaster General relating to air transport, 1926-42. The records concern the administration, organization, and general operation of the airmail service. Each group is arranged by a decimal system.

158. PUBLICITY MATERIALS RELATING TO AIRMAIL SERVICE. 1918-37. 7 ft.
Newspaper clippings; copies of photographs; two post binders of circular letters, schedules, maps of airmail routes, and announcements issued by local post offices; three post binders of photographs concerning airmail displays for use in corridors, at conventions, and in windows; one post binder of blotters pertaining to airmail service; and one post binder of maps and charts on which airmail routes are shown. The newspaper clippings are arranged chronologically; the material in each post binder is arranged alphabetically by State.

159. CORRESPONDENCE AND REPORTS RELATING TO "NATIONAL AIR MAIL WEEK." 1938-39. 5 ft.
"National Air Mail Week," instituted to commemorate the 20th anniversary of the inauguration of regular airmail service, was celebrated from May 15 to May 21, 1938. The records consist mainly of the report of a San Francisco postal inspector; correspondence with airlines, organizations, Air Mail Service assistant superintendents, and Government agencies; correspondence relating to publicity, newsreels, philatelists, pilots, and radio; correspondence of Charles P. Graddick, Superintendent of the Division of Air Mail Service, with the Eaton Paper Corporation; and some correspondence of the Postmaster General. Included are Special Flight Forms 2702A and 2715, which give the route of the flight, departure time, name of pilot, numbers of pouches and pieces of mail carried, and weight of mail. Arranged alphabetically by State.

160. PERFORMANCE AND EFFICIENCY RE-
PORTS ON DOMESTIC AIRMAIL SERVICE.
Aug. 1920-May 1924, May 1931-Apr. 1941.
45 vols. and unbound papers. 21 ft.
  In three groups as follows: (1) Reports,
1920-24 (45 vols.), containing weather data,
information on flight performance (plane number, name of pilot, terminal points of flight,
times of departure and arrival, time in transit,
and number of pouches and weight in pounds of
mail received at start of flight and delivered at
end of flight), efficiency rating (percentage
earned for start, speed, forced landings, and
damage), average efficiency rating for entire
trip, miles flown on trip, forced landing record
(place, time, cause, damage, and disposition
of mail), and percentage of trips completed. The
volumes are arranged chronologically; within
each volume the contents are arranged alphabetically by name of air-transport company.
(2) Reports, 1931-41 (on Form 2718 and un-
numbered forms), showing route number,
location of route, number of trips scheduled,
number of trips arriving at end of route, causes
of delays, and performance records (canceled
and partial flights, completed trips, and miles
flown). Arranged in two groups, one chronologically by month and the other alphabetically by
name of air-transport company. (3) Delayed
operations correction reports, 1934-39, showing
amount and cause of delay. Arranged by name
of air-transport company.

161. RECORDS RELATING TO NATIONAL AIR
TRANSPORT, INC. 1926. 4 in.
  National Air Transport, Inc., carried
airmail in the Middle West under contract with
the Post Office Department before 1927. The
records include performance records of the
company; copies of editorial comment; balance
sheets; a list of stockholders in the company;
endorsements by civic organizations; and information relating to shop equipment, fields, and
hangars. Arranged by subject as listed.

162. BLUEPRINTS AND SPECIFICATIONS FOR
AIRPLANES, PARTS, AND HANGARS.
1918-25. 13 ft.
  Arranged in rough chronological order.

163. MAPS AND PLANS OF LANDING FIELDS.
1918-25. 56 items. 1/2 in.
  Annotated photoprocessed maps and plans.
Arranged in rough chronological order.

164. MAPS SHOWING LANDING FIELDS AND
AIRMAIL ROUTES. 1918-41. 28 items.
1/2 in.
  Published and annotated maps, including
a sketch map that shows the first airmail routes
between New York and Washington, D. C., New
York and Cleveland, and Cleveland and Chicago
and compares the air routes with railroad routes
between these points.

165. PHOTOGRAPHIC PRINTS. 1920-35.
400 items. 2 ft.
  Included are prints showing airplanes, air-
plane accidents, safety devices, airports, and
pilots of the airmail service, and terminals,
equipment, and personnel of Pan American
Airways.

RECORDS OF THE BUREAU OF THE THIRD ASSISTANT POSTMASTER GENERAL

  A Third Assistant Postmaster General was
appointed in accordance with provisions of an
act of June 2, 1836 (5 Stat. 80), to provide more
effectively for the settlement of the accounts of
the Post Office Department. He was assigned
the supervision of the newly established Inspection Office, which was authorized to review and
report on mail-service contracts and to supervise postmasters. Letters commenting on the
efficiency of contractors and the quarterly postage accounts of postmasters were directed to
this office. In 1846 the Office of the Third Assistant Postmaster General was made responsible for all financial operations of the Post Office
Department not delegated to the Auditor by law.
Many of the Third Assistant's inspection duties
were then transferred to the Office of the Chief
Clerk.
  As the postal service expanded in the latter
half of the 19th century, the work of the Office
of the Third Assistant Postmaster General became more varied. In addition to a Division of
Finance, the Office set up divisions to handle
dead letters; issue stamps, stamped envelopes,
newspaper wrappers, and postal cards; manage
the money order, parcel post, postal savings,
and registered mail systems; and classify
mail matter. The Office of the Third Assistant
and its subordinate organizational units became
known collectively as the Bureau of the Third
Assistant Postmaster General in the 1920's.
  The Bureau of the Third Assistant Postmaster General was redesignated the Bureau of
Finance on August 20, 1949, in accordance with
the President's Reorganization Plan No. 3.
  The records of the Bureau of the Third
Assistant Postmaster General that are in the
National Archives--including fiscal records that
predated the Bureau--are arranged according to
the Bureau's organization at the time of the

redesignation. Most of the extant records of the Divisions of Postal Savings, Letters and Miscellaneous Mail, and Registered Mail are at the Post Office Department or at the Washington National Records Center.

RECORDS OF THE DIVISION OF FINANCE

The Division of Finance was established by the Postmaster General in 1872 to handle the receipt and disbursement of postal revenues.

166. GENERAL CORRESPONDENCE. 1922-37. 4 ft.
Chiefly letters received, copies of letters sent, and reports of postmasters relating to the deposit of postal funds in national and State banks. Included are notifications by the Treasury Department of banks in receivership and correspondence concerning lockbox rentals, responsibility for stolen post office funds, safekeeping of stamps and money order forms, and postmasters' checks returned because of insufficient funds. Arranged alphabetically by name of State and thereunder chronologically.

167. ACCOUNTS OF THE GENERAL POST OFFICE IN PHILADELPHIA AND OF THE VARIOUS DEPUTY POSTMASTERS ("LEDGER OF BENJAMIN FRANKLIN"). July 26, 1775-Jan. 5, 1780. 1 vol. 2 in.
This volume contains the accounts of Benjamin Franklin, Richard Bache, Ebenezer Hazard, and Samuel Osgood, who served as Postmasters General under the Continental Congress, and the accounts of deputy postmasters. The latest entry for accounts still open in July 1776 is dated January 1780. Arranged chronologically.

168. LEDGERS OF THE GENERAL POST OFFICE. 1782-1803. 7 vols. 9 in.
In three groups. (1) Five general ledgers: (a) May 1, 1782-March 10, 1790; (b) July 1, 1783-January 21, 1794; (c) October 1, 1793-December 31, 1796; (d) January 1, 1795-December 31, 1799; and (e) for New York, October 19, 1789-November 16, 1790, for Philadelphia, January 3, 1791-August 30, 1797, and for Trenton, September 1797. (These five volumes show accounts of the Postmaster General, the Assistant Postmaster General, deputy postmasters, mail-route contractors, and post riders. The accounts relate to compensation, quarterly accounts, commissions, postage, mail-service contracts, contingent expenses, letters sent by foreign or coastwise ships, incidental expenses, and drafts.) (2) A ledger of errors in quarterly reports by deputy postmasters, July 1, 1799-

October 1, 1803. (3) A cash ledger, October 19, 1789-June 30, 1796. (This volume contains information relating to expenditures for salaries of post office clerks, operating needs, mail contracts, and money received from deputy postmasters.) Within each group the records are arranged chronologically; records in the second group are arranged thereunder alphabetically by name of post office.

169. JOURNALS OF THE GENERAL POST OFFICE. 1782-1801. 2 vols. 3 in.
One volume contains a "General Journal" dated February 2, 1782-July 25, 1790, and a "Cash Book" dated September 25, 1792-October 22, 1795. The other volume contains a "Miscellaneous Journal," dated July 1, 1795-March 28, 1801.

170. LEDGER OF POSTAGE ACCOUNTS OF POST OFFICES WITH THE GENERAL POST OFFICE. July 1785-Jan. 1786. 1 vol. 1 in.
Contains information about paid, unpaid, undercharged, overcharged, way, dead, and ship (coastwise and foreign) letters; letters remaining in post offices; letters missent and later forwarded; and salaries. Arranged chronologically.

171. CORRESPONDENCE RELATING TO SPECIMEN SALARY CHECKS, DRAFTS, AND WARRANTS. Aug. 1916; Feb. 1933-Sept. 1938. 1 in.
Relates to the printing and handling of forms for checks, drafts, and warrants. Included are some undated samples of the forms for 1880-1938. Arranged for the most part chronologically.

RECORDS OF THE POSTAL SAVINGS SYSTEM

172. CORRESPONDENCE REGARDING SUGGESTIONS FOR THE IMPROVEMENT OF THE POSTAL SAVINGS SYSTEM. 1913-20. 1 ft.
The Postal Savings System began in 1913. The records are arranged chronologically.

173. ANNUAL REPORTS. 1913-36. 1 ft.
Arranged chronologically.

174. RECORDS RELATING TO POST OFFICE BOXES (LOCKBOXES). 1894-1934. 1 ft.
Mainly correspondence, memoranda, reports, and tables. Included are memoranda on the regulations governing the use of the boxes, correspondence containing suggestions for improving the service, postmasters' reports on box rentals and key deposits, and tables of rental fees.

RECORDS OF THE DIVISION OF MONEY ORDERS

The domestic postal-money-order system was established on November 1, 1864, within the Office of the Postmaster General. The program was transferred to the jurisdiction of the First Assistant Postmaster General on July 16, 1892, where it was administered by the Division of Money Orders. On December 1, 1905, it was transferred to the Third Assistant Postmaster General. The functions of the Division include the general direction of the money-order system, both domestic and international, and the preparation of conventions for the exchange of money orders with foreign countries.

175. GENERAL RECORDS. 1868-1936. 6 ft.

Correspondence, memoranda, sample forms, and reports of the Division. The correspondence and memoranda relate to difficulties encountered in obtaining funds with which to cash money orders during the Panic of 1907; money order redemptions for prisoners of war; embezzlement, counterfeiting, and forgery of money orders; money orders issued and paid in foreign countries; and money orders mailed to foreign countries during the moratorium of 1933. Sample forms include those used for postal savings banks in foreign countries and those suggested by employees and the public for use in connection with proposed systems of domestic postal savings banks. The reports deal with the electrical accounting system for the issuance, recording, and redemption of money orders; the decrease in money order business as a result of raising the fees in 1925; and the cost of money order business during the depression of the 1930's. Arranged by subject.

176. RECORDS OF INTERNATIONAL MONEY ORDER CONVENTIONS. July 1873-May 1903. 3 ft.

Mainly correspondence between postal officials of the United States and foreign countries concerning conventions for the exchange of money orders. Included are copies of conventions, with proposed amendments and changes; pamphlets and circulars listing regulations governing money order issuance and redemption; lists of foreign offices handling money orders; specimen copies of money order forms; and correspondence relating to foreign exchange rates. Arranged alphabetically by country and thereunder chronologically.

177. MONEY ORDER CONVENTIONS WITH FOREIGN COUNTRIES. 1870-1962. 2 ft.

Conventions for the reciprocal recognition of money orders issued for payment. Arranged alphabetically by name of country.

RECORDS OF THE DIVISION OF STAMPS

The Division of Stamps was established by the Postmaster General in 1872. Its functions include the general supervision of the production and distribution of postage-stamp paper.

178. PLATE PROOF SHEETS OF STAMPS. 1870-97. 6 vols. 1 ft.

Approximately 27,000 certified plate proof sheets of postage stamps made by the Bureau of Engraving and Printing. The proofs include commemorative and ordinary postage, airmail, postage-due, postal savings, newspaper, and parcel post stamps. The proofs are on permanent loan to the Smithsonian Institution. The records are arranged by type and thereunder by number.

179. "STAMP BILL BOOKS." 1870-97. 6 vols. 1 ft.

Contain monthly statements of purchases of ordinary postage, commemorative, specimen, postage-due, special delivery, newspaper, and periodical stamps; stamped envelopes; newspaper wrappers; registered-package envelopes; letter-sheet envelopes; and postal cards. Also included are lists of contractors who furnished postal supplies, statements showing the cost of stamps and supplies, memoranda on the method of disbursing supplies, and a recapitulation of purchases made for the years 1879-97. Arranged chronologically.

180. LEDGER. 1898-1900. 1 in.

Shows quantities and costs of postage stamps, postal cards, stamped envelopes, and newspaper wrappers furnished to Cuba, Puerto Rico, the Philippine Islands, and Guam. Arranged chronologically.

181. RECORDS OF THE POSTAL CARD AGENT. 1893-1923. 2 ft.

A Postal Card Agent was appointed in 1893 by the Postmaster General to inspect and issue postal cards. The United States Postal Card Agency was located for short periods at Birmingham, Conn., Castleton, N.Y., Piedmont, W. Va., and Rumford Falls, Maine. In 1910 the Agency was moved to Washington, D.C., and the Postal Card Agent was designated the Post Office Inspector in Charge of Postal Cards. The records consist chiefly of correspondence, together with related reports, memoranda, and circulars. The correspondence relates to personnel of the Postal Card Agency, contracts for paper and postal cards, defective postal cards, shipments, chemical analysis of paper used, locks and tags used for shipments, and postal card plates, dyes, and inks. Arranged chronologically.

RECORDS OF THE DIVISION OF NEWSPAPER AND PERIODICAL MAIL

The Division of Newspaper and Periodical Mail was established in November 1943 as a successor to the Division of Classification. Its main function is the classification of matter admissible to the mails.

182. RECORDS RELATING TO AN INCREASE IN SECOND-CLASS POSTAGE RATES. Apr. 1917-May 1920. 3 in.

Chiefly correspondence with Members of Congress, postal officials, private companies, fraternal organizations interested in the second-class mailing privilege, and charts, tables, and graphs showing the effect of a proposed increase in rates on the Department's revenue. Also included are memoranda, reports, and circulars relating to the increase. The congressional correspondence is arranged chronologically.

RECORDS OF THE DIVISION OF PARCEL POST

The Parcel Post Service was established on January 1, 1913, within the Office of the Postmaster General. To supervise the Service the Postmaster General, on November 22, 1930, established the Division of Parcel Post within the Bureau of the Third Assistant Postmaster General.

183. RECORDS RELATING TO PARCEL POST FACILITIES IN FOREIGN COUNTRIES. Sept. 1911-Jan. 1912. 5 ft.

Bulletins, booklets, and memoranda relating to parcel post rules, regulations, and rates in foreign countries. These were obtained in countries with a parcel post service by diplomatic officers of the United States in response to a State Department circular dated August 24, 1911, and were transmitted to the Postmaster General. Parcel post information was received from Australia, Austria, Germany, Great Britain, Guatemala, Haiti, Hungary, Luxemburg, Mexico, Morocco, the Netherlands, Portugal, Russia, San Salvador, Spain, Switzerland, and Venezuela. Arranged alphabetically by country.

RECORDS OF THE BUREAU OF THE FOURTH ASSISTANT POSTMASTER GENERAL

The Office of the Fourth Assistant Postmaster General was established by order of the Postmaster General on August 1, 1891, in accordance with provisions of the Appropriation Act of March 3, 1891 (26 Stat. 944). Three divisions were established within the Office to carry out the duties of supervising the establishment of new post offices; of appointing, bonding, and commissioning postmasters; of operating the inspection service; and of investigating mail depredations. The increasing volume of work performed by the Post Office Department made necessary the development of additional services and divisions, and about 1930 the Office of the Fourth Assistant Postmaster General became a Bureau.

As most of the records described here were created before a reorganization of 1946, they are arranged according to the organization existing during the early part of that year. Records of the Division of Rural Mails, however, which had been transferred to the Bureau of the First Assistant Postmaster General in 1929, are described as part of the records of the Fourth Assistant.

On August 20, 1949, the Bureau of the Fourth Assistant Postmaster General was abolished by the President's Reorganization Plan No. 3; and a Bureau of Facilities, under an Assistant Postmaster General, was created to continue the functions of the Bureau.

The most important functions of the Bureau of the Fourth Assistant Postmaster General in 1949 were (1) the administration, operation, and maintenance of Government-owned post office buildings; (2) the authorization of allowances for rent, light, and fuel for post offices and other postal quarters, and allowances for hiring vehicles required for collection and special delivery services; (3) the custody and distribution of equipment and supplies for the Postal Service; (4) the supervision of the screen wagon, pneumatic tube, and Government-owned motor vehicle services; (5) the production and distribution of post-route maps and parcel-post-zone keys; and (6) the supervision of mail equipment shops, and the manufacture and repair of mailbags, locks, keys, and key chains.

RECORDS OF THE IMMEDIATE OFFICE OF THE FOURTH ASSISTANT POSTMASTER GENERAL

The Office consisted of the Fourth Assistant Postmaster General, a deputy, a special administrative aide, assistants, and secretaries.

The main duties of the Office were (1) the supervision and administration of the operations of the Bureau and of its field offices, (2) the review and approval of budget estimates and of journals and allowances from appropriations relating to the Bureau, and (3) the supervision of departmental and field personnel. The Fourth Assistant Postmaster General represented the Postmaster General at Government conferences and on Federal committees relating to public buildings.

184. GENERAL RECORDS. 1905-32. 34 ft.

Letters received and copies of letters sent, memoranda, cost and work reports, committee reports, reports on investigations, statements, and instructions relating to the operation of the Bureau and of its divisions and offices. Arranged by classification number.

185. CORRESPONDENCE OF JAMES I. BLAKSLEE. 1914-20. 1 ft.

Mr. Blakslee served as Fourth Assistant Postmaster General from March 17, 1913, to March 14, 1921. The correspondence relates to the appointment of postmasters, clerks, and rural mail carriers; post office quarters; rural mail service; and deliveries of farm produce by motor vehicle service. Arranged alphabetically by name of correspondent.

RECORDS OF THE DIVISION OF TOPOGRAPHY

The appointment of a clerk to act as topographer of the Post Office Department was authorized by an act of July 2, 1836. The Office of the Topographer, originally under the Chief Clerk, was redesignated the Division of Topography on December 1, 1905, and was transferred from the Office of the Postmaster General to the Bureau of the Fourth Assistant Postmaster General. On July 1, 1913, the Division was absorbed by the Division of Supplies. In accordance with a 1953 order of the Postmaster General, the Division of Supplies was divided into the Division of Equipment and Supplies and the Division of Topography. These Divisions are parts of the Bureau of Facilities, as the Bureau of the Fourth Postmaster General has been known since 1949.

Although the Division of Topography is mainly responsible for compiling, drawing, revising, printing, and distributing post-route maps (State, county, rural delivery, and airmail), it also prepares special-purpose maps and organizational and fiscal charts.

186. LETTERS SENT. Oct. 15, 1901-Sept. 1, 1911. 1 vol. 2 in.

Chiefly press copies of letters and memoranda relating to the organization of the Office of the Topographer and to budget estimates and expenditures, personnel, techniques of reproducing post-route maps, advertisement of proposals for reproducing and furnishing post-route maps, and the acquisition of supplies and equipment. Included are annual and progress reports of the Office of the Topographer and lists of rural delivery service maps. Arranged chronologically.

187. REPORTS OF SITE LOCATIONS. 1865-1946. 292 ft.

Completed forms submitted by postmasters, giving the location of their post offices and other geographical information, to aid the Post Office Department in the preparation of postal maps. The forms contain the official name of the post office, with local name or name changes; section, township, range, and meridian in which the post office was located; terminals of the nearest postal route; mileage to the adjacent post offices, rivers, and creeks; number of feet or rods to the nearest railroad tracks, railroad depot, or highway; and a diagram or map of the location of the post office. The series includes a few reports dated as early as 1837 and as late as 1950. Arranged alphabetically by State, thereunder alphabetically by county and post office, and thereunder by date of report.

188. ATLAS OF POSTAL MAPS. 1839. 13 sheets. 1 in.

A published record copy of The American Atlas Exhibiting the Post Offices, Railroads, Canals, and the Physical and Political Divisions of the United States of America Constructed . . . Under the Direction of the Post Master General by David H. Burr, Geographer to the House of Representatives of the U.S. The atlas contains maps of the United States and adjacent countries, and maps of the following States portrayed singly or in combination: Maine, New Hampshire, Vermont, Massachusetts, Rhode Island and Connecticut, New York, New Jersey and Pennsylvania, Virginia, Maryland and Delaware, North and South Carolina, Georgia and Alabama, Florida, Mississippi, Louisiana and Arkansas, Ohio and Indiana, Kentucky and Tennessee, Illinois and Wisconsin, and Michigan and part of Wisconsin Territory.

189. POST-ROUTE MAPS. 1867-94. 47 items.
      6 in.

An incomplete published set of intermediate-
scale maps of sections of the United States. The
maps were created under the direction of the
Topographer of the Post Office Department. They
show post offices, distances between offices,
frequency of service, and mail-carrying railroads
by name of railroad and include county
boundaries and principal drainage features.
They usually include from two to six States, territories, or parts of States and territories.
Many of the maps have been corrected by hand
and the date of the correction is written on the
map. Arranged chronologically by date of publication. The maps are listed chronologically in
appendix IV. They antedate the post-route
(State) maps described in entry 190 and are different in format. Similar maps of this and
earlier periods are among the cartographic records in Record Group 77, Records of the Office
of the Chief of Engineers.

190. POST-ROUTE (STATE) MAPS. 1894-
      1960. 448 items. 3 ft.

Published maps of individual States, territories, and island possessions of the United
States, on an intermediate scale, showing information relating to post offices, postal routes,
mail-carrying railroads, rural delivery routes,
airmail routes, mail supply points, and method
and frequency of postal service, as well as county
boundaries and principal drainage features.
This series of maps, although different in format, is a continuation of the series described in
entry 189 and was designed to include all editions
of a given map. It is incomplete, however, for
the years before 1937. Some of the editions of
the maps, particularly for the years 1917 and
1935-40, have been annotated to show navigable
waters and coastal waters, and congressional
districts (see also entries 193 and 198). Arranged alphabetically by State, territory, or
island possession and thereunder chronologically by date of publication.

191. MANUSCRIPT MAPS. 1901-47. 63 items.
      2 in.

Manuscript post-route maps of States,
territories, and island possessions, which were
used to prepare the published post-route maps.
Changes were made as necessary on the manu-
scripts, and each one is correct as of the last
date appearing on it. (Some of the earlier maps,
however, are not dated.) These maps show
essentially the same detail as the published post-
route maps described in entry 190. Arranged
alphabetically by State or area. These maps are
listed in appendix V.

192. POSTAL-ZONE MAPS. 1913. 124 items.
      1 in.

A series of published official parcel post
maps of the United States, with annotations of
unknown date showing boundaries of zones used
to determine parcel post charges. These maps
were prepared for use with the parcel-post guide.
There is also a map annotated to show parcel
post unit areas within each State. The maps are
arranged by zone number.

193. POST-ROUTE (STATE) MAPS SHOWING
      NAVIGABLE WATERS. 1917. 14 items.

Published post-route maps of States mainly
in the eastern United States, annotated with information relating to the navigable waters in the
particular State and to the coastal waters of those
States bordering on the Atlantic Ocean and the
Gulf of Mexico. Arranged alphabetically by name
of State.

194. CITY MAPS. 1912-35. 575 items. 3 ft.

Published, photoprocessed, and manuscript
maps of selected cities in the United States, annotated with information apparently relating to
delivery routes and locations of postal facilities,
business sections, sidewalks, and mail boxes.
Arranged by case number, thereunder alphabetically by State, and thereunder alphabetically
by city.

195. RURAL-DELIVERY-ROUTE MAPS.
      1927-28. 600 items. 1 ft.

A representative sampling of the maps
prepared to show rural delivery routes throughout the United States. These maps--generally
annotated blueprints--are each accompanied by
a carbon typescript of the official description of
the route, giving the stops to be made, the distance between each stop, and the total mileage
of the route. Arranged alphabetically by name
of post office.

196. RURAL-DELIVERY-ROUTE LOCAL-
      CENTER MAPS. 1900-37. 600 items.
      1 ft.

Manuscript maps of rural areas throughout the United States, showing the rural delivery
routes servicing the areas. Arranged alphabetically by State.

197. RURAL-DELIVERY-ROUTE COUNTY
      MAPS. n.d. 40 items. 3 in.

An incomplete set of photoprocessed maps,
probably of the 1930's, showing rural delivery
routes. Arranged alphabetically by State and
thereunder by county.

198. POST-ROUTE (STATE) MAPS SHOWING
      CONGRESSIONAL DISTRICTS. 1935-40.
      58 items. 4 in.
        An incomplete set of published post-route
maps annotated to show the boundaries and the
numbers of the congressional districts within
the individual States. Arranged alphabetically
by State and thereunder chronologically by date
of publication of the base map.

199. POST-ROUTE (STATE) MAPS ANNOTATED
      WITH RED DOTS. 1935-40. 63 items.
      4 in.
        Published post-route maps, with annota-
tions in the form of red dots over certain cities
or towns. There is no key to these dots, which
appear to have been placed on the maps by hand.
They may identify first-class post offices. Arranged alphabetically by State and thereunder
chronologically by date of publication of the
base map.

200. POST-ROUTE (STATE) MAPS ANNO-
      TATED WITH NUMBERS. 1937-39.
      3 items.
        Published post-route maps stamped with
6-digit numbers, usually along railroad routes.
No key is given to these numbers. Arranged
alphabetically by State.

RECORDS OF THE DIVISION OF
MOTOR VEHICLE SERVICE

        Although there was an experimental auto-
mobile mail-collection service in Milwaukee,
Wis., in February 1908, motor vehicle service
was not authorized by Congress until its inclu-
sion in the postal appropriations for the fiscal
year 1915. This service and the screen wagon
service (mail carried by wagon and later by
motortruck enclosed by a steel screen) were assigned to the Division of Post Office Services in
the Bureau of the First Assistant Postmaster
General on July 1, 1916. In September 1921 the
work relating to the operation of the Government-
owned motor vehicle service and the contract
vehicle service was transferred to the newly
created Division of Vehicle Transportation in
the Bureau of the Fourth Assistant Postmaster
General. The Division was redesignated the
Division of Motor Vehicle Service on October 6,
1921, and was transferred back to the Bureau
of the First Assistant. During the latter part
of 1930 the Division was reassigned to the Bureau of the Fourth Assistant Postmaster General.
The Division was mainly concerned with the
operation of the Government-owned motor
vehicle service and the pneumatic tube service.

201. GENERAL RECORDS. 1858-1939. 9 ft.
        Advertisements, contracts, and corre-
spondence concerning the construction and operation of mail transportation vehicles. Also
included are materials relating to the claim of
H. C. McFarlin of Little Rock, Ark., under a
screen-wagon contract. The records are arranged in rough chronological order.

202. CORRESPONDENCE RELATING TO THE
      SHIPMENT OF FARM PRODUCE BY
      POSTAL MOTORTRUCK SERVICE. 1919-
      29. 1 ft.
        Chiefly interoffice memoranda and corre-
spondence with postmasters, route agents, Members of Congress, farmers, and merchants.
Arranged alphabetically by name of commodity.

RECORDS OF THE
PNEUMATIC TUBE SERVICE

        The transportation of mail by pneumatic
tubes was initiated in 1893 in Philadelphia with
the construction of an experimental line of 6-inch
tubes between the Main Post Office and the East
Chestnut Street Station. Because of demands to
extend the service in Philadelphia and to establish it in other cities, the Post Office Department in 1900 appointed a local and a general
committee to investigate the advisability of extending the service; and a formal report was
submitted to Congress on January 4, 1901. The
use of the service was authorized by an act of
April 21, 1902. Since July 1, 1904, provisions
for pneumatic tube service contracts for Boston,
New York City, Brooklyn, Chicago, and St. Louis
have been included in the annual appropriations
for the Post Office Department.

203. GENERAL RECORDS. 1892-1919. 27 ft.
        Correspondence, reports, and contracts
relating to the establishment and operation of
the pneumatic tube service; correspondence concerning the invention and ownership of pneumatic
tubes; correspondence, surveys, studies, and
blueprints relating to the extension of the service from the New York General Post Office to a
station in Brooklyn, and from the Boston General
Post Office to the North Postal Station, the
South Terminal Railroad Station, the Essex
Street Postal Station, and the Back Bay Station.
Also included are statistics on the weight of
mail delivered; reports on the proposed extension
of services; advertisements for and correspondence related to bids to carry mails by pneumatic
tubes; maps and blueprints of the routes to be
used; and reports on the installation of air-cooling

apparatus in the Boston General Post Office. Arranged by subject as listed.

204. **REPORTS AND CORRESPONDENCE RE- GARDING THE PNEUMATIC TUBE SERVICE.** 1908-51. 8 ft.
Included are exhibits. Arranged in rough chronological order.

205. **ORDERS.** 1902-6. 1 vol. 1 in.
Original orders authorizing the establishment, change, or discontinuance of pneumatic tube service in Boston, New York City, Philadelphia, Chicago, and St. Louis. The orders include the name of the contractor, names of stations along the route, mileage between stations, rate of pay per mile, and total amount paid per year. Also included are advertisements for contracts, proposals for carrying the mails by pneumatic tubes or similar devices, and instructions to bidders. Arranged by route number.

206. **RECORDS CONCERNING A COURT OF CLAIMS CASE REGARDING PNEUMATIC TUBES.** 1903-53. 7 ft.
Relate to U.S. Court of Claims Case No. 162-5 between the New York Transportation Co. and the Post Office Department. Included are transcripts of hearings, reports, and conclusions. Arranged in rough chronological order.

207. **RECORDS OF THE PNEUMATIC TUBE COMMISSION.** 1912-14. 1 ft.
The Commission To Investigate Pneumatic Tube Postal Systems, usually known as the Pneumatic Tube Commission, consisted of two members of the House, two members of the Senate, and the Second Assistant Postmaster General, Joseph Stewart. It was established by Congress on August 24, 1912, to investigate the desirability of Government ownership of the pneumatic tube service then operated under contract in New York, Boston, Chicago, Philadelphia, Brooklyn, and St. Louis. The Commission's records include its minutes and final report; reports, memoranda, and photographs relating to the operation of the pnuematic tube service; correspondence and memoranda on related patents; and copies of contracts.

RECORDS OF THE DIVISION OF POST OFFICE QUARTERS

The responsibility for post office quarters not in Government-owned buildings was shared by the Office of the Postmaster General, the Solicitor for the Post Office Department, the Chief Inspector, and the Supervising Architect of the Treasury Department until June 10, 1933, when Executive Order 6166 assigned the responsibility to the Division of Building Operations and Supplies of the Bureau of the Fourth Assistant Postmaster General. In October 1933 the Postmaster General ordered this function transferred to the newly created Division of Post Office Quarters.

This Division leased or rented quarters for post offices, post office garages, and railway terminals; authorized allowances for rent and for light, fuel, water, and equipment required in such quarters; and reviewed reports prepared by postal inspectors relating to the quarters.

208. **GENERAL RECORDS.** 1916-42. 3 ft.
Correspondence, reports, and exhibits relating to an alleged combination among equipment companies to control prices; correspondence and reports relating to the maintenance and construction of post offices; administrative issuances; and divisional work-progress reports. Arranged by subject or type of record.

209. **RECORDS RELATING TO LEASES.** 1916-32. 3 ft.
Postal inspectors' reports relating to the valuation of postal quarters (post offices, stations, branches, terminals, and garages); postmasters' reports about local leases; hearings of a Senate committee on post office leases; correspondence and reports concerning leases for the St. Paul Commercial Station and Chicago Post Office; architectural specifications and floor plans of the Boston Back Bay Station and the Chicago Federal Building; and a 1916-25 register of leases approved by the Solicitor for the Post Office Department. Arranged by type of record and thereunder chronologically.

210. **BLUEPRINTS, SKETCH PLANS, AND ESTIMATES FOR THE CONSTRUCTION OF POST OFFICE BUILDINGS OR EXTENSIONS.** 1911-30. 12 ft.
Also included are copies of Form No. 1414, which was prepared by postmasters and which gives information about the space in and condition of Federal buildings and the number of employees in the buildings; questionnaires completed by postmasters on the space accommodations necessary for proposed Federal buildings; a few city maps showing notations of old and proposed postal stations and garages; a few reports on leased property occupied by the Post Office Department; and a few records relating to the construction of the Washington, D.C., City Post

Office in 1912. The records are arranged alphabetically by name of State.

211. RECORDS RELATING TO DEDICATIONS OF POST OFFICE BUILDINGS. 1933-42. 12 ft.

Histories containing descriptions of newly constructed post office buildings, name changes, names of postmasters and dates of their appointments, statements of postal receipts, and dates of establishment, discontinuance, and reestablishment of post offices; correspondence with postmasters and Congressmen relating to dedication ceremonies; copies of dedication speeches; and postal inspectors' reports. Arranged alphabetically by name of State.

RECORDS OF THE DIVISION OF EQUIPMENT AND SUPPLIES

In accordance with an order of the Postmaster General dated November 1, 1905, all clerks in the Post Office Department engaged in handling supplies and in related work were transferred to the Division of Supplies under the Bureau of the Fourth Assistant Postmaster General. The Division administered the appropriation for all supplies purchased and furnished directly to the postal service.

On July 1, 1913, the Division of Equipment, which had operated the mailbag repair shops and the mail-lock shop in Washington, D.C., was transferred from the Bureau of the Second Assistant Postmaster General to the Bureau of the Fourth Assistant Postmaster General and combined with the Division of Supplies. The name of the Division was not changed until October 6, 1921, however, when it became known as the Division of Equipment and Supplies and was made responsible for the manufacture of mailbags. In 1933, by order of the Postmaster General, the Division of Equipment and Supplies was redesignated the Division of Building Operations and Supplies. The former title was restored when the Postmaster General, on June 18, 1943, reorganized the Bureau of the Fourth Assistant Postmaster General.

The Division was mainly concerned with the preparation of specifications for supplies and equipment; the review of bids and subsequent recommendations to purchasing agents; and the receipt, storage, control, and issue of stock and operating equipment.

212. COST REPORTS. 1915-24. 1 ft.

Monthly reports of work performed in mail-equipment shops, showing types of work, number of employees and labor hours, and labor and unit costs for each job. Arranged chronologically.

213. MISCELLANEOUS RECORDS. 1868-1911. 3 ft.

Selected records illustrating the operations of the Division. Included are bids, requisitions, and contracts for equipment and supplies; memoranda relating to proposals for repairing and maintaining post office buildings; applications for positions; letters of recommendation; leave records; lists of employees; and correspondence concerning the disposition of waste material. Interspersed among the other records are references to records of the Disbursing Clerk relating to acknowledgments of checks and vouchers, payrolls, settlement of accounts, estimates of appropriations for repairs, deficiency estimates, contingent expense accounts, and receipts for payments. Arranged chronologically.

RECORDS OF THE DIVISION OF RURAL MAILS

Rural free delivery had been instituted on October 1, 1896. It was established by an act of April 28, 1902, as a branch of the Office of the General Superintendent of Free Delivery within the Bureau of the First Assistant Postmaster General. On May 9, 1903, the Postmaster General transferred the Division of Free Delivery, the Superintendent of City-Free-Delivery Service, and the Superintendent of Rural Free Delivery to the Bureau of the Fourth Assistant Postmaster General. The Office of the General Superintendent of Free Delivery was discontinued on May 27, 1903, and the remaining offices and services of the Division of Free Delivery were organized into separate divisions.

On April 30, 1910, the Postmaster General directed that the star-route functions of the Division of Contracts in the Bureau of the Second Assistant Postmaster General be transferred to the Bureau of the Fourth Assistant and combined with the Division of Rural Free Delivery under the title of Division of Rural Mails. The Division of Rural Mails was responsible for the operation of rural delivery service and for the appointment and supervision of rural mail carriers. The Division was transferred to the Bureau of the First Assistant Postmaster General in 1929, to the Bureau of the Second Assistant Postmaster General in 1932, and back to the Bureau of the First Assistant Postmaster General on July 1, 1942, where it was coordinated with the other delivery services in the Post Office Service.

A description of many of the early records of the Division of Rural Mails can be found in entries 93 and 94.

214. GENERAL RECORDS. 1915-34. 94 ft.

Letters received, copies of letters sent, memoranda, postal inspectors' reports, cost reports, orders, statements, instructions, petitions, and some maps relating to the establishment, extension, and discontinuance of rural mail routes and to the administration of the Division. Arranged in four groups as follows: (1) by classification number, 1922-38; (2) alphabetically by State and thereunder alphabetically by county, 1915-18; (3) alphabetically by State and thereunder alphabetically by post office; and (4) alphabetically by State, 1932-34.

215. RECORDS RELATING TO ACTS PROVIDING FOR FEDERAL AID TO POST ROADS. Sept. 1912-Mar. 1917. 10 in.

Federal aid for the construction and improvement of post roads was provided under the Post Office Department Appropriation Acts of August 24, 1912, and March 4, 1913, and under the Federal-Aid Road Act of July 11, 1916.

The records consist of correspondence with the Department of Agriculture and State and county governments concerning the distribution of funds and plans for the construction, improvement, and relocation of roads; surveys and studies relating to post roads in Alabama, Iowa, and Texas; and a chart showing "Operations on Post Roads Designated for Improvement Under Act of August 24, 1912."

216. FORMS. 1902-10. 2 ft.

Forms used for letters, interoffice and serial memoranda, general orders, instructions,

questionnaires, and lists; and posting media used by the Office of the General Superintendent of Delivery System and the Division of Rural Free Delivery. In three groups: (1) for 1906-10, arranged by form number; (2) for 1902-7, arranged chronologically; and (3) for 1909.

217. RECORDS RELATING TO RURAL MAIL CARRIERS. 1901-20. 11 ft.

Letters received, copies of letters sent, applications, and petitions relating to the eligibility, appointment, reinstatement, transfer, promotion, bonding, and efficiency of rural mail carriers; and correspondence concerning the establishment and discontinuance of rural mail routes, schedules, and changes in routes   In two groups: (1) for 1901-17, arranged alphabetically by name of post office and (2) "State Files-Appointment Section," for 1913-20, arranged alphabetically by name of State and thereunder chronologically.

218. ACCOUNTING RECORDS. 1906-19. 4 vols. 4 in.

Representative accounting records, including (1) accounts of rearrangements, amendments, and discontinuances in the rural delivery service, 1906-8; (2) accounts of various items paid (service, substitutes, clerks in rural stations, tolls, and ferriage) from the general appropriation for rural delivery service, village delivery service, and star service, 1908-16; (3) accounts for travel and miscellaneous expenses in the postal service office of the Fourth Assistant Postmaster General, for clerks in charge of substations, for rural carriers, and for toll and ferriage, 1906-7; and (4) accounts of star payments by the New York, Chicago, and San Francisco subtreasuries, 1917-19. Arranged in the order listed.

RECORDS OF THE BUREAU OF ACCOUNTS

The Office of the Comptroller of the Treasury, by an act of September 2, 1789 (1 Stat. 66), was made responsible for the compilation of audits and the settlement of accounts for the General Post Office. These accounting functions were transferred to the Fifth Auditor of the Treasury on March 3, 1817 (3 Stat. 366), and to the Sixth Auditor on July 2, 1836 (5 Stat. 81).

The functions remained within the Treasury Department until the Bureau of Accounts was established in the Post Office Department, in accordance with the Budget and Accounting Act of June 10, 1921 (42 Stat. 24). The Bureau, comprising a Headquarters Office (also known as the Office of the Comptroller) and the

Accounts, Cost Ascertainment, and Methods and Procedures Divisions performed the following duties: (1) examining all accounts of salaries and incidental expenses, all postal and money order accounts of postmasters, and accounts relating to the transportation of mail; and (2) certifying quarterly to the Postmaster General an accounting of postmasters' funds and of the general expenses of the postal service. The General Accounting Office audited and preserved these accounts, in compliance with legislation regarding the fiscal operations of the Government.

The Bureau of Accounts was terminated by the Postmaster General on June 12, 1953. Its functions were at that time transferred to a newly established Bureau of the Controller, which was terminated on November 1, 1954. The functions are now assigned to the Bureau of Finance.

219. GENERAL RECORDS. 1889-1924.
23 ft.

Letters received, copies of letters sent, memoranda, reports, statements, bulletins, and lists. Arranged alphabetically by subject and thereunder chronologically.

220. LETTERS SENT. 1904-18. 20 vols.
2 ft.

Press copies of letters of the Auditor of the Treasury for the Post Office Department concerning mainly personnel and audits of postal accounts. Interspersed among the letters are lists of employees, the indebted postal accounts of postmasters, requisitions for repairs and supplies, and inventories of equipment. Arranged chronologically.

221. SEA POST OFFICE ACCOUNTS. 1891-
1914. 1 vol. 1 in.
Arranged chronologically.

222. GENERAL POST OFFICE ACCOUNTS
WITH FOREIGN COUNTRIES. 1883-86,
1892-1903. 3 vols. 4 in.
Arranged by name of country and thereunder chronologically.

223. CLOSED TRANSIT STATEMENTS WITH
FOREIGN COUNTRIES. 1893-98. 1 vol. 1 in.
The statements were prepared when bulk mail was sent to a foreign country without being opened enroute. Arranged alphabetically by country and thereunder chronologically.

224. POSTAL-MONEY-ORDER ACCOUNTS
WITH FOREIGN COUNTRIES. July-
Aug. 1914. 4 vols. 8 in.
Arranged alphabetically by country and thereunder chronologically.

225. RECEIPTS OF PAYMENT FOR FOREIGN
MAIL TRANSIT BY SEA. 1900-1909.
3 vols. 3 in.
Arranged alphabetically by country and thereunder chronologically.

226. RECORDS OF PAYMENT OF MONEY
ORDER ACCOUNTS WITH FOREIGN
COUNTRIES. 1911-15. 2 vols. 4 in.
Arranged alphabetically by country and thereunder chronologically.

227. POSTMASTERS' ACCOUNTS. 1862-74.
360 vols. 30 ft.
Arranged alphabetically by State, thereunder alphabetically by city, and thereunder chronologically.

RECORDS OF THE BUREAU OF THE CHIEF INSPECTOR

From the time the Post Office Department was established, the Postmaster General employed the Assistant Postmasters General as special agents to investigate the operations of post offices. As early as June 14, 1790, the Postmaster General prepared detailed instructions for reporting on irregularities discovered during visits to post offices. The supervision of this activity was assigned at about this time to the Office of Instructions in the Office of the Postmaster General. In 1830 the Office of Instructions was redesignated the Office of Instructions and Mail Depredations and was made part of the Office of the Second Assistant Postmaster General.

From 1835 to 1939 the responsibility for the supervision of investigations of mail depredations was transferred by the Postmaster General, successively, to the following units: Miscellaneous Division, Office of the Postmaster General; Contract Division, Office of the Second Assistant Postmaster General; Office of Mail Depredations, Office of the Postmaster General; Division of Special Agents and Mail Depredations, Office of the Postmaster General; Division of Post Office

Inspectors and Mail Depredations, first in the Office of the Postmaster General and later in the Office of the Fourth Assistant Postmaster General; and the Division of Post Office Inspectors, Office of the Postmaster General.

On February 2, 1939, the Postmaster General established the Bureau of the Chief Inspector, comprising the Office of the Chief Inspector and the Administrative Investigations, Mail Investigations, and Financial Investigations Divisions. The Bureau was authorized to investigate all matters relating to mail depredations; to consider complaints of criminal offenses against the postal service; to handle claims for rewards granted for the prosecution of offenders against postal laws; to supervise the Post Office Inspection Service; and to inspect the finances, property, and equipment of the Post Office Department.

The director of the inspection agents of the Post Office Department was known during various periods as the Chief Post Office Inspector, Division Superintendent, Division Chief, Chief Special Agent, and Chief Inspector. When the Bureau of the Chief Inspector was organized in 1939, the

Chief Inspector's functions included the general supervision of the Bureau and the Post Office Inspection Service; the development and administration of inspection policies and programs; the selection, assignment, and separation of departmental and field personnel of the Bureau; and the maintenance of liaison with the National Archives, the Army, and the Navy.

228. LETTERS SENT BY THE CHIEF SPECIAL AGENT, OFFICE OF MAIL DEPREDATIONS. May 21, 1875-July 11, 1877. 1 vol. 2 in.

Press copies of letters sent to special agents of the Inspection Division in the field, to postmasters, and to other postal officials relating to irregularities in receiving, handling, and dispatching mail. Arranged chronologically. The volume is indexed by name of person, by post office, and by State.

229. REGISTER OF ARRESTS FOR OFFENSES AGAINST POSTAL LAWS. Aug. 1864-Jan. 1876; Jan. 1878-May 1897. 13 vols. 2 ft.

Shows date of arrest, name of prisoner, official position, where and by whom arrested, alleged offense, and remarks. In some cases the disposition of the case is written in over the entry. Entries are arranged chronologically. Each volume is indexed by name of person arrested.

230. INDEX TO ARRESTS. Jan. 1, 1888-Dec. 31, 1891; Jan. 1, 1895-June 30, 1899. 3 vols. 6 in.

Shows the names of the prisoner and arresting agent and the date and place of arrest. Each volume is divided into two parts: the first part is arranged alphabetically by the first letter of the surname; the second, alphabetically by field office division.

231. CASE FILES OF INVESTIGATIONS. Nov. 1877-Dec. 1903. 157 ft.

Correspondence, reports, memoranda, and other records relating to individual violators of postal laws and regulations. A typical file includes the report of arrest, a photograph of the violator, correspondence with post office inspectors explaining the nature of the violation, the report of indictment, exhibits, newspaper clippings, and a report of the result of the trial and the final disposition. The records for November 1877-June 1899 are arranged chronologically; those for June 1800-December 1903 are arranged numerically. A name index to the case files has been retained by the Office

of the Chief Inspector. A case file relating to a mail robbery in 1838 is at the beginning of the series.

232. STATEMENTS OF ARRESTS. Jan. 1881-Dec. 1890. 1 vol. 2 in.

Concern post office employees arrested for violations of postal laws. Each statement shows the date of arrest, name and official position of the violator, where and by whom arrested, the offense, and remarks. Arranged chronologically by month.

233. RECORDS RELATING TO THE RAILWAY MAIL SERVICE INVESTIGATION. Feb.-May 1925. 1 ft.

Mainly correspondence and reports of an investigation of the 15 divisions of the Railway Mail Service, conducted in April and May 1925 in response to a request of February 3, 1925, from the Second Assistant Postmaster General. The reports pertain to the status of work, methods of operation, and morale of employees and include suggestions for improving the service. A copy of the letter of February 3, 1925, and a memorandum of instructions to inspectors are filed at the beginning of the series.

234. ROSTERS. 1898-1909. 1 ft.

Rosters of post office inspectors and clerks at Division headquarters, showing the dates of original appointments, dates of promotions, salaries, States where employed, methods of appointment, and (where applicable) travel commission numbers. Arranged chronologically.

235. ANNUAL REPORTS. 1905-35. 2 ft.

Submitted by the Office of the Chief Inspector to the Postmaster General. Included are correspondence and exhibits pertaining to the preparation of the reports. Arranged chronologically.

236. BIMONTHLY GENERAL INTELLIGENCE PRESS REPORTS OF THE JUSTICE DEPARTMENT. Nov. 1918-Jan. 1921; Mar. 1921-May 1922. 1 ft.

Concern the activities of the radical press in the United States. Each report is indexed by name of publication or organization mentioned. Arranged chronologically.

237. RECORDS OF THE INSPECTION OFFICE, ST. LOUIS, MO. Sept. 28, 1876-June 3, 1878. 2 vols. 4 in.

Chiefly press copies of letters and reports from the Special Agent in Charge to the Chief Special Agent, Inspection Office, Washington, D.C., and other post office officials. The records concern mail depredations, post office personnel, and administrative matters. Arranged chronologically. Each volume is indexed by name of post office.

238. RECORDS OF THE INSPECTION OFFICE, DENVER, COLO. Dec. 20, 1879-May 8, 1907. 32 vols. 5 ft.

Press copies of records sent by the Post Office Inspector in Charge to the Chief Postal Inspector, Washington, D.C., and by special agents in Nebraska, New Mexico, Utah, and Wyoming to the Post Office Inspector in Charge of the Denver Division. They comprise (1) evaluations of inspections of the star, rural, messenger, and money order services and of post offices; (2) special reports on post office construction, postmasters, mail contractors, rural mail carriers, postal clerks, and stagecoach robberies; (3) requests for postal stationery and lockboxes; (4) diagrams of proposed post office locations; and (5) case reports concerning evasion of postage charges, fraudulent use of the mail, tampering with registered mail, post office robberies, burning of post offices, and postmasters' embezzlements. Arranged chronologically.

239. RECORDS OF THE INSPECTION OFFICE, PHILADELPHIA, PA. May 12, 1896-July 21, 1909. 34 vols. 6 ft.

Press copies of records sent by the Post Office Inspector in Charge to the Chief Postal Inspector, Washington, D.C., and by the special agent and Rural Mail Delivery District Supervisor, Pittsburgh Division, to the Post Office Inspector in Charge of the Philadelphia Division. The records comprise (1) Forms 567-D, 567-E, 567-F, 568-A, 573-A, 573-K, and 576-A, which relate to arrests and preliminary hearings, indictments, results of trials, validity of postmaster's bonds, irregularities at post offices, recommendations to remove postal employees, and evaluations of post office inspections; and (2) reports and descriptions of rural routes from postal inspectors, which concern such subjects as evasion of postage charges, fraudulent use of the mails, tampering with registered mail, post office robberies, mail losses, burning of post offices, and mutilation of mail. Arranged chronologically.

240. RECORDS OF THE INSPECTION OFFICE, NEW YORK, N.Y. Apr. 27-May 28, 1907; Sept. 10-Oct. 7, 1908. 2 vols. 4 in.

Mainly press copies of correspondence and reports sent by the Post Office Inspector in Charge to the Chief Postal Inspector, Washington, D.C. The records include (1) Forms 573b, showing the condition of post office accounts; (2) form letters approving bonds issued to postmasters; and (3) case reports from field postal inspectors concerning the evasion of postage charges, fraudulent use of the mails, tampering with registered mail, post office robberies, mail losses, burning of post offices, and mutilation of mail. Arranged chronologically.

APPENDIXES

I. Functions Under the Jurisdiction of the First Assistant Postmaster General, 1789-1950

Functions carried on by the First Assistant Postmaster General in 1950 were in general continued by his successor, the Assistant Postmaster General in charge of the Bureau of Post Office Operations.

General Management

Allowances to post offices for clerks and for rent, fuel, light, and other items: 1864-91, 1905-50.

City free delivery system and appointment of carriers: 1863-May 1903, Dec. 1905-1950.

Rural delivery service: Oct. 1896-May 1903, 1929-34, 1943-50.

Auditing accounts of postmasters: 1789-May 1810, May 1810-May 1830 (post offices in northern half of United States only), May 1830-July 1836.

Payment of mail contractors: 1789-May 1810, May 1810-May 1830 (contractors in northern half of United States only), May 1830-Oct. 1851.

Inspection of post roads: 1789-1810.

Establishment and maintenance of mail routes (advertising, receiving bids, arranging schedules, preparing contract papers): May 1810-May 1830 (routes in northern half of United States only), July 1836-Oct. 1851.

Transmission of mailbags, mail locks, and keys: July 1836-1842.

Ocean mail steamship service: 1855-69.

Appointment and removal of route and local agents: 1855-88.

Foreign mail service: 1850-July 1868.

Appointment of railway postal clerks and mail messengers: 1874-88.

Money order system: 1898-1905.

Issuance to postmasters of blanks, wrapping paper, twine, and miscellaneous items: 1810-30, Oct. 1851-1891, Dec. 1905-1950.

Airmail service: 1939-41.

Government-owned motor vehicles: 1916-Sept. 1921, July 1923-July 1929.

Establishment of Post Offices

Establishment and discontinuance of post offices: 1800-May 1810, May 1810-May 1830 (post offices in northern half of United States only), Mar. 1833-July 1836, Oct. 1851-Aug. 1891, Dec. 1905-1950. (Discontinuance and changes of sites of fourth-class post offices were handled by the Fourth Assistant Postmaster General from 1911 to 1915.)

Selecting, equipping, and leasing quarters for Presidential post offices: 1923-29.

Establishment, maintenance, and discontinuance of contract stations: 1917-50.

Appointment of Postmasters

Appointing postmasters and issuing bonds, oaths, and commissions: 1800-May 1810, May 1810-May 1830 (post offices in northern half of United States only), Mar. 1833-July 1836, Oct. 1851-Aug. 1891, Dec. 1905-1950.

Readjustment of salaries of postmasters: 1864-91, 1905-50.

Treatment of Dead Letter Mail

Treatment of dead letter mail: July 1891-Dec. 1905. Feb. 1915-1950.

II. Changes in the Organization of and Services Furnished by the Bureau of the Second Assistant
Postmaster General, 1841-1950

The organizational units and services within the Bureau of the Second Assistant Postmaster
General are listed as nearly as possible in the order of their establishment. If the exact date of
establishment cannot be ascertained, approximate dates are given. Some organizational units or
services apparently merged with others or were informally discontinued, with the result that no
terminal dates could be given. This list does, however, give a general picture of the organization
of and the services furnished by the Bureau.

Topography Division
        Established on July 2, 1836
        Transferred to the Bureau of the First
        Assistant Postmaster on July 1, 1913

Powerboat or "Steamboat" Service
        Established in 1841
        Supervised by the Office of Railway Mail
        Service from 1864
        Supervised by the Division of Surface Postal
        Transport from 1946
        Supervised by the Highway and Contract
        Transportation Division from 1950

Star Route Service
        Established on Mar. 3, 1845
        Supervised by the Contract Division about
        1851
        Consolidated with the Division of Rural
        Mails, Bureau of the Fourth Assistant
        Postmaster, on Oct. 1, 1910
        Supervised by the Division of Railway Mail
        Service, Bureau of the Second Assistant
        Postmaster, from July 8, 1929
        Supervised by the Division of Surface
        Postal Transport from 1946
        Supervised by the Highway and Contract
        Transportation Division from 1950

International Postal Service Division
        Established as the "foreign desk" in 1850;
        supervised by the Office of the Postmaster
        General
        Supervised by the Bureau of the First
        Assistant Postmaster from 1857
        Division of Foreign Mails established on
        July 27, 1868
        Supervised by the Office of the Postmaster
        General from 1879
        Supervised by the Bureau of the Second
        Assistant Postmaster from July 20, 1891
        Name changed to Division of International
        Postal Service on July 7, 1928
        Name changed to Division of International
        Postal Transport Service in 1946
        Name changed to Division of International
        Service in 1950

Contract Division
        Established as "Contract Office" about 1851
        Name changed to Contract Division in the
        period 1873-76
        Discontinued in 1910

Railway Post Office Service
        Established on July 7, 1862
        Incorporated with the Division of Railway
        Mail Service on July 1, 1907

Inspection Division
        Established about 1865
        Discontinued in 1910

Mail Messenger Service
        Established in 1869
        Supervised by the Division of Miscellaneous
        Transportation from 1910
        Supervised by the Bureau of the First
        Assistant Postmaster from July 1, 1916
        Supervised by the Bureau of the Second
        Assistant Postmaster in the 1920's
        Supervised by the Division of Surface Postal
        Transport from 1946
        Supervised by the Highway and Contract
        Transportation Division from 1950

Railway Mail Service Division
        Established as the Division of Railway Mail
        Service in 1873
        Name changed to Division of Surface Postal
        Transport in 1946
        Name changed to Railway Transportation
        Service Division in 1950

Division of Equipment
        Established as the Mail Equipment Division
        in the period 1873-76
        Name changed to Division of Equipment on
        July 1, 1900
        Supervised by the Bureau of the Fourth
        Assistant Postmaster from July 1, 1913

Special Agents and Mail Depredation Division
        Established in the period 1873-76
        Discontinued in the period 1877-78

II.--Continued.

Railway Classification Division
    Established in the period 1877-78
    Discontinued in the period 1879-90

Division of Railway Adjustments
    Established in 1878
    Name changed to Division of Administrative
        Services in 1946
    Name changed to Transportation Accounts
        Division in 1950

Inland and Foreign Mail Boat Service
    Established in the period 1879-90

Special Office Service
    Established during the 1880's

Electric Line and Cable Car Service
    Established during the 1890's

Ocean Mail Service
    Established on Mar. 3, 1891
    Supervised by the Division of Foreign Mails

Sea Post Service
    Established in 1891
    Supervised by the Division of Foreign Mails
    Discontinued on Feb. 9, 1942

Screen Wagon Service
    Established about 1892
    Transferred to the Bureau of the First
        Assistant Postmaster in 1916

Pneumatic Tube Service
    Established about 1892
    Transferred to the Bureau of the Fourth
        Assistant Postmaster about 1904

New York Harbor Boat Service
    Established in 1896

Division of Rural Mail Service
    Established in 1896 as the Office of Rural
        Free Delivery
    Supervised by the Bureau of the First
        Assistant Postmaster from Apr. 28, 1902
    Name changed to Division of Free Delivery
        and supervised by the Bureau of the Fourth
        Assistant Postmaster on May 9, 1903
    Name changed to Division of Rural Free
        Delivery on May 27, 1903
    Name changed to Division of Rural Mails
        on Apr. 30, 1910
    Supervised by the Bureau of the First
        Assistant Postmaster from 1929

Supervised by the Bureau of the Second
    Assistant Postmaster from 1932
Supervised by the Bureau of the First
    Assistant Postmaster from July 1, 1942
Supervised by the Bureau of Post Office
    Operations after 1950

Alaska Mail Service
    Established about 1898

Division of Miscellaneous Transportation
    Established in 1910
    Discontinued in 1916

Terminal, Side, and Transfer Service
    Established in the period 1910-20

Government-Owned Motor Vehicle Service
    Established in 1914

Government-Operated Star Route Service
    Established in 1917

Division of Air Mail Service
    Established as a Government-owned and
        Government-operated service on Nov. 15,
        1918; contract service from Sept. 1, 1927
    Supervised by the Bureau of the First
        Assistant Postmaster from Aug. 8, 1938
    Supervised by the Bureau of the Second
        Assistant Postmaster from July 2, 1940
    Transferred from field service to depart-
        mental service on July 1, 1944
    Name changed to Division of Air Postal
        Transport in 1946
    Name changed to Air Service Division in
        1950

Contract Vehicle Service
    Established in 1919

Foreign Airmail Service
    Established on Oct. 19, 1927
    Supervised by the Division of Foreign Mails
        after 1927
    Supervised by the Division of Air Postal
        Transport from 1946
    Supervised by the Division of Air Service
        from 1950

Highway Post Office Service
    Established on July 11, 1940

Budget and Administrative Services
    Supervised by the immediate office of the
        Second Assistant Postmaster, particularly

II.--Continued.

   the office of the Special Administrative
    Aide, before 1946
   Supervised by the Division of Administra-
    tive Services from 1946
   Supervised by the Budget and Administra-
    tive Services Division from 1950

Motor Transportation Service
  Established in 1947

Helicopter Airmail Service
  Established in 1947

Highway and Contract Transportation Division
  Established in 1950

III. List of Postal Conventions and Agreements Among the Records of the Bureau of the
Second Assistant Postmaster General (Entry 141)

The list is arranged alphabetically by name of the country or of the colony with which the agreement or convention was concluded. The multilateral conventions are given at the end of the list.
The date shown is usually the date of signing at the time the convention was concluded.

Bilateral Conventions and Agreements

Argentina
>   Parcel post convention, Mar. 15, 1915

Australia. See New South Wales, Queensland,
and Tasmania.

Austria
>   Parcel post convention, Oct. 9, 1908

Bahamas
>   Postal conventions, Dec. 19, 1887, and
>   Dec. 23, 1914

Barbados
>   Postal conventions, Nov. 10, 1887, and
>   Mar. 13, 1915

Belgium
>   Postal convention, July 17, 1858; additional
>   articles to, July 31, 1863
>   Postal convention, Aug. 21, 1867; detailed
>   regulations for execution of, Jan. 15, 1868;
>   additional convention to, Mar. 1, 1870;
>   second additional convention to, May 12,
>   1873
>   Agreement for increasing limits for weight
>   and size of merchandise samples exchanged
>   by post, Feb. 7, 1882
>   Additional agreement, Mar. 30, 1922, to
>   parcel post convention of Nov. 19, 1904

Bermuda
>   Postal convention, Aug. 9, 1876

Bolivia
>   Agreement, Nov. 13, 1901, to make cor-
>   rections to the parcel post convention of
>   Apr. 24, 1900, and to sign anew
>   Parcel post convention, Jan. 9, 1908
>   Amendment, Nov. 10, 1908, to parcel post
>   convention of Nov. 30, 1901

Brazil
>   Postal convention, Mar. 14, 1870
>   Parcel post convention, Mar. 26, 1910;
>   ratification of, May 29, 1911

Bremen
>   Arrangements for handling U.S. mail,
>   Sept. 13, 1847

Postal conventions, Aug. 4, 1853; May 17,
1855; 1860 (not signed); Aug. 23 and
Nov. 28, 1860; and Mar. 28, 1864

British Columbia
>   Postal convention, June 9, 1870

British Guiana
>   Parcel post convention, Feb. 3, 1892
>   Postal convention, Nov. 20, 1915

British Honduras
>   Postal convention, Feb. 4, 1915
>   See also Honduras.

Canada
>   Articles of agreement, Mar. 25, 1851
>   Additional articles of agreement establishing
>   exchange of postal cards, June 19, 1873
>   Postal arrangement, Jan. 27, 1875; additional
>   articles to, Oct. 26, 1877, and May 3,
>   1881; amended article, Feb. 10, 1882, to
>   replace article 2 of the additional articles
>   of agreement of May 3, 1881
>   Postal convention, Jan. 19, 1888; amend-
>   ments to, Apr. 25, 1888, June 28, 1904,
>   Apr. 1, 1907, and Jan. 7, 1908
>   See also British Columbia and Newfoundland.

Chile
>   Postal convention, signed at Santiago on
>   March 4, at Washington on June 30, and
>   at New York on July 3, 1876; drafts of
>   Draft of ratifications (not signed) of parcel
>   post convention concluded in 1889
>   Parcel post convention, Dec. 6, 1898;
>   amendment to, Sept. 8, 1908
>   Parcel post convention, Nov. 21, 1919

Costa Rica
>   Parcel post convention, Apr. 1, 1890

Cuba
>   Parcel post convention, Oct. 31, 1925;
>   protocol to, Apr. 13, 1927

Danish West Indies
>   Parcel post convention, Oct. 7, 1890

III. --Continued.

Denmark
Postal convention, Nov. 7, 1871; detailed regulations for the execution of; additional articles of agreement to, Sept. 29, 1874
Parcel post conventions, June 30, 1906, and Apr. 28, 1922

Dominican Republic
Postal convention, May 19, 1917

Dutch East Indies. See Netherlands East Indies.

Dutch Guiana
Parcel post convention, Aug. 9, 1909

Dutch West Indies
Postal convention, May 17, 1915

Ecuador
Postal convention, May 9, 1871; ratifications of, Dec. 6, 1871
Parcel post convention, Dec. 28, 1906

Eire. See Irish Free State.

Fiji
Parcel post convention, June 10, 1920

Finland
Parcel post convention, Jan. 12, 1922

France
Parcel post convention, June 15, 1908; document authorizing Postmaster General of the United States to exchange ratifications of, Aug. 7, 1908; protocol of exchange of ratifications of; copy of, bearing ratification of France, July 15, 1908; additional arrangement to, Jan. 15, 1921
Arrangement concerning weight of parcel post packages, Feb. 7, 1911; amendment to, Aug. 1, 1912; additional arrangement to, Jan. 15, 1921
Draft of arrangement concerning establishment of sea post offices (no date)

French Indochina
Parcel post convention, Nov. 8, 1921

Germany
Additional articles of agreement establishing an exchange of postal cards, Oct. 31, 1873
Parcel post convention, Aug. 26, 1899
Parcel post convention, June 25, 1925

Agreement for collect-on-delivery parcel post service, Dec. 22, 1931
See also Bremen, Hamburg, North German Union, and Prussia.

Gibraltar
Agreement concerning parcel post, Dec. 7, 1914

Great Britain. See United Kingdom of Great Britain and Ireland.

Greece
Parcel post convention, July 8, 1913

Guatemala
Postal convention, June 4, 1862
Parcel post conventions, Dec. 4, 1888, and Dec. 4, 1899

Guiana. See British Guiana and Dutch Guiana.

Haiti
Parcel post convention, Feb. 4, 1911

Hamburg
Postal convention, June 12, 1857; additional articles to, Aug. 23, 1860, Nov. 11, 1863, and Mar. 28, 1864

Hawaii
Postal convention, May 4, 1870
Parcel post convention, Dec. 19, 1888

Honduras
Parcel post convention, June 20, 1896
See also British Honduras.

Hong Kong
Postal convention, Aug. 10, 1867

Hungary
Parcel post convention, June 27, 1910

Irish Free State
Article of agreement, Dec. 5, 1927

Italy
Postal convention, July 8, 1863
Postal convention, Nov. 8, 1867; detailed regulations for execution of, Mar. 19, 1868; amended article to replace article 16 of detailed regulations, May 1, 1869; additional convention to the convention, Jan. 16, 1870

Agreement for increasing limits for weight
and size of merchandise samples exchanged
by post, June 6, 1889
Parcel post convention, June 16, 1908

Japan
Postal convention, Aug. 6, 1873; detailed
regulations for execution of, July 15,
1874; additional agreement to, Feb. 8,
1876
Agreement on prepayment of postage,
Apr. 26, 1875; additional agreement to,
Feb. 8, 1876
Parcel post convention, June 30, 1904;
amendments to, Mar. 2, 1909, and
Oct. 10, 1912
Agreements on contents of parcel-post
packages, Nov. 4, 1915, and May 10, 1919

Leeward Islands
Parcel post convention, Apr. 3, 1889
Postal convention, Feb. 13, 1915

Mexico
Postal conventions, Oct. 20, 1884, and
June 21, 1887
Parcel post convention, Apr. 28, 1888;
amendment to, May 25, 1911
Agreement for establishment of system for
handling registered through-mail pouches,
to go into effect on Feb. 15, 1889 (not
executed)
Parcel post convention, Aug. 17, 1917

The Netherlands
Postal convention, Sept. 26, 1867; detailed
regulations for execution of, Nov. 26,
1867; additional convention to the convention, Jan. 10, 1870; amended article to
replace article 16 of detailed regulations,
May 23, 1870; additional article to convention and additional convention, June 19,
1874
Amendment to parcel post convention,
Apr. 22, 1909
Parcel post convention, Nov. 16, 1926

Netherlands East Indies
Parcel post convention, Apr. 3, 1918
Parcel post agreement signed at Batavia
on Oct. 2, 1922, and at Washington on
Feb. 15, 1924

Netherlands Guiana. See Dutch Guiana.

Netherlands West Indies. See Dutch Guiana and
Dutch West Indies.

Newfoundland
Postal convention, Nov. 20, 1872; additional
articles of agreement to, Sept. 15, 1873,
Sept. 22, 1876, and Oct. 23, 1877
Parcel post convention, Jan. 8, 1894
Articles of agreement, Feb. 13, 1909
See also Canada.

New South Wales
Postal convention, Jan. 15, 1874; amended
article to replace article 3 of, June 1, 1875
Postal convention, Dec. 3, 1890

New Zealand
Postal convention, Aug. 3, 1870; amended
article to replace article 3 of, Aug. 28,
1877
Parcel post convention, Feb. 12, 1900
Postal convention, Aug. 30, 1916

Nicaragua
Parcel post conventions, May 18, 1885;
Mar. 27, 1900

North German Union
Postal convention, Oct. 21, 1867; regulations
for execution of, June 30, 1868; additional
article to convention; additional convention,
Apr. 7, 1870, to the convention; additional
article to convention and to additional
convention, Mar. 31, 1871; regulations for
execution of convention and additional convention, June 10, 1870

Norway
Parcel post conventions, Aug. 27, 1904;
Jan. 11, 1921; and Feb. 28, 1929

Panama
Postal convention, June 19, 1905; amendment to, July 19, 1905

Paraguay
Parcel post convention, Dec. 15, 1919

Peru
Parcel post convention, May 28, 1906;
amendment to, Sept. 1, 1908

III.--Continued.

Prussia
      Postal convention, additional articles,
        Aug. 29, 1885
      Additional articles, Dec. 28, 1860, to
        postal convention of July 17, 1852

Queensland
      Postal convention, Dec. 8, 1875

Salvador
      Postal convention, July 20, 1870
      Parcel post convention, July 27, 1917

Siam
      Parcel post convention, Oct. 15, 1921

Spain
      Parcel post convention, Feb. 4, 1921
      Parcel post agreement, Nov. 10, 1931
      Postal convention, Nov. 10, 1931

Straits Settlements
      Parcel post convention, Feb. 24, 1922
      Parcel post agreement, Oct. 20, 1928

Surinam. See Dutch Guiana.

Sweden
      Parcel post conventions, Nov. 14, 1905,
        and Mar. 24, 1922

Switzerland
      Postal convention, Oct. 11, 1867; regula-
        tions for execution of, Nov. 28, 1867;
        additional article to regulations, Mar. 6,
        1869; additional convention to the conven-
        tion, Feb. 7, 1870; second additional
        convention to the convention, May 6, 1872;
        additional articles of agreement to conven-
        tion, Mar. 31, 1874
      Agreement for increasing limits for weight
        and size of merchandise samples exchanged
        by post, Aug. 31, 1882
      Parcel post convention, Dec. 15, 1922

Tasmania
      Postal convention, May 31, 1886

Thailand. See Siam.

Trinidad and Tobago
      Postal convention, Jan. 3, 1918

United Kingdom of Great Britain and Ireland
      Additional articles, Aug. 10, 1853, to con-
        vention of Dec. 15, 1848, to authorize
        exchange of mail between U.S. ports and
        British packet office at Panama

Articles agreed upon for executing convention
  of Dec. 15, 1848; additional articles to
  articles, Dec. 3, 1852, May 19 and Dec. 12,
  1853, Mar. 20, 1856, June 17, 1858,
  Jan. 11 and Nov. 23, 1859, June 28 and
  Aug. 13, 1860, July 7 and Dec. 26, 1862,
  Sept. 26, 1863, Aug. 6, 1864, and Oct. 23,
  1865
Postal convention, June 18, 1867; detailed
  regulations for execution of, Aug. 9, 1867
Postal convention, July 28, 1868
Postal convention, Nov. 7, 1868; detailed
  regulations for execution of; additional
  convention to, Dec. 3, 1869
Postal convention, Aug. 11, 1869
Special arrangement to fix transit charges
  on British closed mails conveyed across
  the United States, Oct. 6, 1876
Agreement for increasing limits for weight
  and size of merchandise samples exchanged
  by post, June 18, 1880
Postal convention, June 4, 1913

Uruguay
      Parcel post convention, Feb. 10, 1908

Venezuela
      Postal convention, July 19, 1865
      Parcel post convention, May 1, 1899

Virgin Islands. See Danish West Indies.

West Indies. See Bahamas, Barbados, Cuba,
  Danish West Indies, Dutch Guiana, Dutch West
  Indies, Haiti, Leeward Islands, and Trinidad
  and Tobago.

Multilateral Conventions and Agreements

Universal Postal Union
      Postal conventions concluded at Paris on
        June 1, 1878 (designated the Lisbon
        Convention); Rome, May 26, 1906; Madrid,
        Nov. 30, 1920; Stockholm, Aug. 28, 1924;
        and London, June 28, 1929
      French ratifications of convention concluded
        at Paris on June 1, 1878
      Spanish-American postal convention signed
        at Madrid on Nov. 13, 1920

Pan American Postal Union
      Principal convention and parcel post con-
        vention concluded at Buenos Aires on
        Sept. 15, 1921
      Principal convention and parcel post con-
        vention concluded at Mexico City on Nov. 9,
        1926

IV. Special List of Post-Route Maps (Entry 189)

"Post Route Map of the States of New Hampshire, Vermont, Massachusetts, Rhode Island, Connecticut and Parts of New York and Maine." Scale 1 inch to 6 miles. 1867.

"Post Route Map of the State of New York and Parts of Vermont, Massachusetts, Connecticut, New Jersey and Pennsylvania. Showing also the adjacent portions of the Dominion of Canada." Scale 1 inch to 6 miles. 1868.

"Post Route Map of the States of Pennsylvania, New Jersey, Delaware and Maryland and of the District of Columbia with adjacent parts of New York, Ohio, Virginia and West Virginia." Scale 1 inch to 6 miles. 1869.

"Post Route Map of the State of Maine and of the adjacent parts of New Hampshire and the Dominion of Canada." Scale 1 inch to 8 1/2 miles. 1873.

"Post Route Map of the States of Michigan and Wisconsin with adjacent parts of Ohio, Indiana, Illinois, Iowa and Minnesota." Scale 1 inch to 10 miles. 1873.

Part of "Post Route Map of the States of Illinois, Iowa and Missouri with adjacent parts of Indiana, Wisconsin, Minnesota, Nebraska, . . . and Arkansas." Scale 1 inch to 10 miles. 1873. Much of Missouri is missing.

"Post Route Map of the States of Pennsylvania, New Jersey, Delaware and Maryland and of the District of Columbia with adjacent parts of New York, Ohio, Virginia and West Virginia." Scale 1 inch to 6 miles. 1873.

"Preliminary Post Route Map of the State of Texas with adjacent parts of Louisiana, Arkansas and Indian Territory." Scale 1 inch to 15 miles. 1874.

Eastern half of "Post Route Map of the State of Texas with adjacent parts of Louisiana, Arkansas, [and] Indian Territory . . . ." Scale 1 inch to 15 miles. 1878. Post routes are not shown.

"Post Route Map of the State of Colorado." Scale 1 inch to 11 miles. 1879.

Post-route map of the States of Virginia, Maryland, and Delaware with parts of adjoining States. Scale 1 inch to approximately 8 miles. 1879.

"Post Route Map of the State of Oregon and Territory of Washington." Scale 1 inch to 12 miles. 1880.

"Post Route Map of the State of Oregon and Territy of Washington." Scale 1 inch to 10 miles. 1883.

"Post Route Map of the States of Pennsylvania, New Jersey, Delaware, and Maryland and of the District of Columbia with adjacent parts of New York, Ohio, Virginia and West Virginia." Scale 1 inch to 6 miles. 1883.

"Post Route Map of the States of Illinois, Iowa and Missouri with adjacent parts of Indiana, Wisconsin, Minnesota, Nebraska, Kansas and Arkansas." Scale 1 inch to 10 miles. 1885.

"Post Route Map of the States of Ohio and Indiana with adjacent parts of Pennsylvania, Michigan, Illinois, Kentucky and West Virginia." Scale 1 inch to 8 miles. 1885.

"Post Route Map of the State of Louisiana with adjacent parts of Mississippi, Arkansas . . . ." Scale 1 inch to 8 5/8 miles. 1885. Dated Oct. 1, 1885.

"Post Route Map of the State of Louisiana with adjacent parts of Mississippi, Arkansas and Texas." Scale 1 inch to 8 5/8 miles. 1885. Dated Dec. 1, 1855.

"Post Route Map of the Territories of New Mexico and Arizona with parts of adjacent States and Territories." Scale 1 inch to approximately 12 miles. 1885.

"Post Route Map of the States of California and Nevada." Scale 1 inch to 12 miles. 1885.

"Post Route Map of the Territories of Montana, Idaho and Wyoming with parts of adjacent States and Territories." Scale 1 inch to approximately 15 miles. 1885.

IV. --Continued.

"Post Route Map of the Territory of Dakota with adjacent parts of Montana, Wyoming, Nebraska, Iowa and Minnesota and portions of the Dominion of Canada." Scale 1 inch to 10 miles. 1885.

"Preliminary Post Route Map of the States of Kansas and Nebraska with adjacent parts of Missouri, Iowa, Dakota, Colorado, Texas and Indian Territory." Scale 1 inch to 10 miles. 1885.

"Post Route Map of the State of Colorado." Scale 1 inch to 10 miles. 1885.

"Post Route Map of the State of Texas with adjacent parts of Louisiana, Arkansas, Indian Territory and of the Republic of Mexico." Scale 1 inch to 15 miles. 1885.

"Post Route Map of the State of Minnesota with adjacent parts of Iowa, Nebraska, Dakota, Wisconsin and of the British Possessions." Scale 1 inch to 10 miles. 1885.

"Post Route Map of the State of Florida with adjacent parts of Georgia and Alabama. Also the neighboring West India Islands." Scale 1 inch to 12 miles. 1885.

"Post Route Map of the States of Pennsylvania, New Jersey, Delaware and Maryland and of the District of Columbia with adjacent parts of New York, Ohio, Virginia and West Virginia." Scale 1 inch to 6 miles. 1885. Corrected to June 1, 1885.

"Post Route Map of the States of Pennsylvania, New Jersey, Delaware and Maryland and of the District of Columbia with adjacent parts of New York, Ohio, Virginia and West Virginia." Scale 1 inch to 6 miles. 1885. Corrected to Dec. 1, 1855.

"Post Route Map of the State of Maine [and parts of New Hampshire and the Dominion of Canada]." Scale 1 inch to 6 1/2 miles. 1886.

"Post Route Map of the States of North Carolina and South Carolina with adjacent parts of Georgia, Tennessee, Kentucky, West Virginia and Virginia." Scale 1 inch to 8 miles. 1886.

"Post Route Map of the Territories of Montana, Idaho and Wyoming with parts of adjacent States and Territories." Scale 1 inch to 15 miles. 1886.

"Post Route Map of the State of Louisiana with adjacent parts of Mississippi, Arkansas and Texas." Scale 1 inch to 8 5/8 miles. 1887.

"Post Route Map of the State of Oregon and Territory in Washington." Scale 1 inch to 10 miles. 1887.

"Post Route Map of the States of North Carolina and South Carolina with adjacent parts of Georgia, Tennessee, Kentucky, West Virginia and Virginia." Scale 1 inch to 8 miles. 1887.

"Post Route Map of the Territories of Montana, Idaho and Wyoming with parts of adjacent States and Territories." Scale 1 inch to 15 miles. 1887.

"Post Route Map of the States of Kentucky and Tennessee with parts of adjacent States." Scale 1 inch to 8 miles. 1887.

"Post Route Map of the State of New York and parts of Vermont, Massachusetts, Connecticut, New Jersey and Pennsylvania. Also the adjacent portions of the Dominion of Canada." Scale 1 inch to 6 miles. 1887.

"Post Route Map of the State of New York and parts of Vermont, Massachusetts, Connecticut, New Jersey and Pennsylvania. Also the adjacent portions of the Dominion of Canada." Scale 1 inch to 6 miles. 1890.

"Post Route Map of the States of Oregon and Washington with adjacent parts of Idaho, Nevada, California and British Columbia." Scale 1 inch to 10 miles. 1891.

"Post Route Map of the States of Montana, Idaho and Wyoming with parts of adjacent States and Territories." Scale 1 inch to 12 miles. 1891. Corrected to May 1, 1891.

IV.---Continued.

"Post Route Map of the States of Montana, Idaho and Wyoming with parts of adjacent States and Territories." Scale 1 inch to 12 miles. 1891. Corrected to June 1, 1891.

"Post Route Map of the State of Arkansas and of Indian and Oklahoma Territories with adjacent portions of Mississippi, Tennessee, Missouri, Kansas, Texas and Louisiana." Scale 1 inch to 10 miles. 1891.

"Post Route Map of the State of Georgia and Outline Map of South Carolina with adjacent parts of North Carolina, Tennessee, Alabama and Florida." Scale 1 inch to 10 miles. 1894.

"Post Route Map of the States of New Hampshire, Vermont, Massachusetts, Rhode Island, Connecticut and parts of New York and Maine." Scale 1 inch to 6 miles. 1894. Part of the map is missing.

Post-route map of parts of Virginia, Kentucky, Tennessee, North Carolina, and South Carolina. n. d.

Post-route maps of parts of Alabama, Georgia, and Florida. Two editions, n. d.

V. List of Manuscript Post-Route Maps (Entry 191)

Alabama: 1943
Alaska: 1939
Arizona: ca. 1910, 1947
Arkansas: 1939
California and Nevada: 1938
Canal Zone: Not dated
Colorado: 1942
Connecticut: See Massachusetts.
Cuba: Not dated
Delaware. See District of Columbia.
District of Columbia, Maryland, and Delaware:
    Not dated
Florida: 1942
Georgia: 1939
Idaho: 1933. See also Montana.
Illinois: 1940 (two copies)
Indiana: 1933
Iowa: ca. 1910, 1934
Kansas: 1937
Kentucky: 1929
Kentucky and Tennessee: 1910 (two copies)
Louisiana: ca. 1910, 1947
Maine: 1939
Maryland. See District of Columbia.
Massachusetts, Rhode Island, and Connecticut:
    1935
Michigan: 1941
Michigan and Wisconsin: ca. 1910
Minnesota: 1934
Mississippi: 1941
Missouri: 1942
Montana: 1939
Montana, Idaho, and Wyoming: ca. 1910

Nebraska: 1938
Nevada. See California.
New Hampshire. See Vermont.
New Jersey: 1937
New Mexico: 1943
New York: 1935
New York: Long Island, not dated
North Carolina: 1932
North Dakota: 1932
Ohio: ca. 1910
Oklahoma: 1937
Oregon: 1928
Pennsylvania: 1945
Pennsylvania: Philadelphia and vicinity, not dated
Pennsylvania: Pittsburgh and vicinity, 1944
Philippine Islands: Not dated
Puerto Rico: 1936
Rhode Island. See Massachusetts.
South Carolina: ca. 1910, 1936
South Dakota: 1932
Tennessee: 1938. See also Kentucky.
Territory of Hawaii: 1923
Texas: 1937
Texas: Dallas-Fort Worth area, 1937
Utah: 1939
Vermont and New Hampshire: 1941
Virginia. See West Virginia.
Washington: 1941
Washington: Seattle and vicinity (two maps), not
    dated
West Virginia and Virginia: ca. 1910, 1939
Wisconsin: 1943. See also Michigan.
Wyoming: 1940. See also Montana.

☆ U.S. GOVERNMENT PRINTING OFFICE : 1984 O - 451-718

www.ingramcontent.com/pod-product-compliance
Lightning Source LLC
Chambersburg PA
CBHW081546040426
42448CB00015B/3241